21.75

Calculated to Please 3
Calculator activities for the National Curriculum

GW00602827

Paul Harling

——— UNWIN HYMAN ———
SKILLS AND RESOURCES SERIES

"CALCULATOR METHODS

The attainment targets and programmes of study in mathematics demonstrate a recognition that calculators provide a powerful and versatile tool for pupils to use in both the development of their understanding of number and for doing calculations. Calculators are now an established item of classroom equipment, and should be available for pupils to use at all four key stages.

They provide a fast and efficient means of calculation, liberating pupils and teachers from excessive concentration on pencil and paper methods. By increasing the options available to pupils, by enabling more ambitious exploration of numbers to be undertaken, and by saving time in making calculations, calculators offer an opportunity to increase standards of attainment.

In learning to use calculators, pupils should have the opportunity to:
- become familiar with the number operations to be performed by calculators as they progress through the levels of Attainment Targets 2 and 3;
- explore the way a calculator works through a variety of number games and similar activities;
- develop confidence in selecting correct key sequences for various calculations;
- use mental methods to estimate for expected answers, check for reasonableness and interpret results;
- use calculators as a powerful means of exploring numbers and to extend their understanding of the nature of numbers and number relationships."

National Curriculum Non-Statutory Guidelines: Mathematics (paras 4·0–4·3)

Thanks to Texas Instruments for supplying calculators for the front cover.

Published in 1990 by
UNWIN HYMAN LIMITED
15/17 Broadwick Street
London W1V 1FP

© Paul Harling 1990

British Library Cataloguing in Publication Data

Harling, Paul
Calculated to please
1. Schools. Curriculum subjects
Mathematics, Teaching aids Electronic calculators
I. Title
510'.7'8

ISBN 0 0444 8143 8

Designed by Pete Lawrence
Illustrated by Trevor Ricketts
Typeset by Cambridge Photosetting Services
Produced by AMR, Basingstoke
Printed in Great Britain by
Alden Press Ltd., Oxford
and bound by Hunter & Foulis Ltd., Edinburgh

Teachers' guide

Introduction

The three books in this series constitute a wide-ranging collection of activities which involve children in the use of electronic calculators as a fundamental part of their mathematical education in the primary years. As the *National Curriculum Proposals* point out, 'it is essential that all pupils leave school knowing how to use a calculator effectively'. (*National Curriculum Proposals* para. 3.33; 1988.)

The series is designed to complement and be used as part of the existing mathematics scheme(s) of your school, and has a numerical and conceptual content that is closely matched to all the major mathematics schemes currently available. It is *not* a comprehensive scheme for the teaching of arithmetical skills and concepts through the use of calculators. Rather, it contains a series of activities, games, problems and investigations in which the calculator can be clearly seen to be an *aid* to the child in his or her learning. It is always possible for children to use pencil and paper to work out an arithmetical problem and, in fact, there are few curricular or 'real-world' situations in which a calculator is essential to the child. It is likely, therefore, that some children could work through almost all the pages in this series without recourse to a calculator! However, there are a number of benefits to be gained from calculator use at all stages of primary education.

1 There is immediate feedback to the child about the correctness or otherwise of his or her work. This important asset of calculator use can give many children increased confidence in their abilities. Related to this is the fact that early indication of mistakes can prevent their reinforcement as the child proceeds through a page or section of a scheme.

2 Calculators are a significant motivator for children of all ages. As in all school subjects and activities, there are some aspects of mathematics which are relatively tedious. The calculator can help to reduce the burden of routine computation and induce a more positive attitude to mathematics in general.

3 Related to the last point is the fact that the reduction in the burden of arithmetic can have a very beneficial effect on two aspects of work, namely the attention span of the child, which is always increased by the use of calculators, and the ability of the child to concentrate on the purpose of the activity with a reduced tendency to be side-tracked into 'number crunching'.

4 Proficiency with calculators allows the child to use realistic numbers reliably in problem solving. In this way the child's ability to estimate, round and approximate quantities can be greatly enhanced.

5 It is likely that the use of calculators will occasionally throw up a concept which is new to the child. Such situations might involve, for example, the production of a negative number or an interesting decimal in the display. The door is then open for you to discuss the concept in a context actually created by the child and therefore of significant interest to him or her.

6 Similar to the above is the situation which often arises in the use of calculators for the teaching of money. The classical example is the way in which the calculator will show 50p or £0·50 as 0.5 when producing this amount as the 'answer' in the display. Lack of understanding of the link may indicate a lack of understanding of place value, the notation of money, or both. These can then be explored further in a child-orientated context. The calculator can therefore be of significant use to the teacher as a tool of diagnosis, which is so essential in formative assessment and evaluation of learning.

Contents

Title	Mathematical content
27 Changing places	Place-value changes when dividing repeatedly by 10.
28 1089 or not?	Number investigation.
29 Come to the point	Ratios (fractions) which produce common decimals.
30 Figure skating	Ordering, adding and dividing decimals.
31 Party planner	Problem solving.
32 Memory	Using the calculator memory.
33 Ferry good money!	Problem solving.
34 Hop-scotch	Game involving estimation, rounding, addition and subtraction of decimals.
35 Larger or smaller	Multiplication of decimals.
36–40 Twister (+, −, ×, ÷)	Decimal place value: all four operations.
41 A bunch of three	Ordering fractions and decimals.
42 Divide and match	Patterns in fraction families.
43–44 Repeaters 1 and 2	Patterns of recurring decimals.
45–48 Use your calculator	Using a calculator in measurement activities: length, area, mass, volume and capacity.

CALCULATED TO PLEASE BOOK 3

	National Curriculum Level 3	National Curriculum Level 4	National Curriculum Level 5
AT 1 **Using and applying mathematics** Use number, algebra and measures in practical tasks, in real life problems, and to investigate within mathematics itself	• select the materials and the mathematics to use for a task; check results and consider whether they are sensible. • explain work being done and record findings systematically. • make and test predictions.	• select the materials and the mathematics to use for a task; plan work methodically. • record findings and present them in oral, written or visual form as appropriate. • use examples to test statements or definitions.	• select the materials and the mathematics to use for a task; check there is sufficient information; work methodically and review progress. • interpret mathematical information presented in oral, written or visual form. • make and test simple statements.
	Calculated To Please Activities 1 2 3 4 5 6 7 8 9	**Calculated To Please Activities** 10 11 12 13 14 15 16 17 18 19 20 21 22 23 24 25 26 27 28 29 30	**Calculated To Please Activities** 31 32 33 34 35 36 37 38 39 40 41 42 43 44 45 46 47 48
AT 2 **Number** Understand number and number notation	• read, write and order numbers to at least 1000; use the knowledge that the position of a digit indicates its value • use decimal notation as the conventional way of recording in money. • appreciate the meaning of negative whole numbers in familiar contexts.	• read, write and order whole numbers. • understand the effect of multiplying a whole number by 10 or 100. • use, with understanding, decimal notation to two decimal places in the context of measurement. • recognise and understand simple everyday fractions. • recognise and understand simple percentages. • understand and use the relationship between place values in whole numbers.	• use index notation to express powers of whole numbers. • use unitary ratios
	Calculated To Please Activities 1 2 3 4 5 6 7 8 9 16	**Calculated To Please Activities** 10 11 12 14 15 16 17 18 19 20 21 22 23 24 25 26 27 28 29 30 31 32 33 36 37 38 39 40 45 46 47 48	**Calculated To Please Activities** 41 42 43 44
AT 3 **Number** Understand number operations (addition, subtraction, multiplication and division) and make use of appropriate methods of calculation	• know and use addition and subtraction number facts to 20 (including zero). • solve problems involving multiplication or division of whole numbers or money, using a calculator where necessary. • know and use multiplication facts up to 5 × 5, and all those in 2, 5 and 10 multiplication tables.	• know multiplication facts up to 10 × 10 and use them in multiplication and division problems. • (using whole numbers) add or subtract mentally two 2-digit numbers; add mentally several single-digit numbers; without a calculator add and subtract two 3-digit numbers, multiply a 2-digit number by a single-digit number and divide a 2-digit number by a single-digit number. • solve addition or subtraction problems using numbers with no more than two decimal places; solve multiplication or division problems starting with whole numbers.	• (using whole numbers) understand and use non-calculator methods by which a 3-digit number is multiplied by a 2-digit number and a 3-digit number is divided by a 2-digit number. • calculate fractions and percentages of quantities using a calculator where necessary. • multiply and divide mentally single-digit multiples of powers of 10 with whole number answers. • use negative numbers in context.
	Calculated To Please Activities 1 3 7 8 9 10 12	**Calculated To Please Activities** 3 4 5 6 7 8 9 10 11 13 14 15 17 18 19 20 21 22 23 24 26 27 28 29 30	**Calculated To Please Activities** 16 22 28 30 31 32 33 34 35 36 37 38 39 40 41 42 43 44 45 46 47 48

AT 4 **Number** Estimate and approximate in number	• recognise that the first digit is the most important in indicating the size of a number, and approximate to the nearest 10 or 100. • understand 'remainders' given the context of calculation, and know whether to round up or down. **Calculated To Please Activities** 1 2 3 7 8 9 10	• make use of estimation and approximation to check the validity of addition and subtraction calculations. • read a calculator display to the nearest whole number. • know how to interpret results on a calculator which have rounding errors. **Calculated To Please Activities** 2 4 5 6 7 8 9 11 12 16 17 18 19 20 21 22 23 24 29 30 32 41	• use and refine 'trial and improvement' methods. • approximate using a specified number of significant figures or decimal places. **Calculated To Please Activities** 24 25 26 27 28 29 30 31 32 33 34 35 41 42 43 44 45 46 47 48
AT 5 **Number/Algebra** Recognise and use patterns, relationships and sequences and make generalisations.	• explain number patterns and predict subsequent numbers where appropriate. • find number patterns and equivalent forms of 2-digit numbers and use these to perform mental calculations. • recognise whole numbers which are exactly divisible by 2, 5 and 10. **Calculated To Please Activities** 1 2 3 4 5 6 7 8 9 10	• apply strategies, such as doubling and halving, to explore properties of numbers, including equivalence of fractions. • generalise, mainly in words, patterns which arise in various situations. **Calculated To Please Activities** 11 12 13 14 15 16 17 18 19 20 22 23 24 25 26 27 28 29 33	• understand and use terms such as prime, square, cube, square root, cube root, multiples and factors. • recognise patterns in numbers through spatial arrangements. • follow simple sets of instructions to generate sequences. **Calculated To Please Activities** 15 16 21 22 28 29 30 31 32 34 35 36 37 38 39 40 42 43 44 45 46 47 48
AT 6 **Algebra** Recognise and use functions, formulae, equations and inequalities	• deal with inputs to and outputs from simple function machines. **Calculated to Please Activities** 1 2 3 4 5 6 7 8 9 16	• understand and use simple formulae or equations expressed in words. • recognise that multiplication and division are inverse operations and use this to check calculations. **Calculated To Please Activities** 10 11 12 13 14 15 16 17 18 19 20 21 22 23 24 25 26 27 29 35 36 37 38 39 40 42	• understand and use simple formulae or equations expressed in symbolic form. • express a simple function symbolically. **Calculated To Please Activities** 15 28 30 31 32 33 41 42 43 44 45 46 47 48

The target users of *Calculated to Please*

Calculated to Please is a series of three books, each containing about 40 activities.

Book 1 has been designed for use with children in the infant age range of 5 to 7 years. It concentrates on keyboard skills, general familiarity with the calculator, and work in addition and subtraction of whole numbers.

Book 2 has been designed for use with younger junior children between the ages of 7 and 9 years. It concentrates on general arithmetical work with whole numbers, including the skills of estimation, simply investigations and items of problem solving.

Book 3 has been designed for use with older junior or middle-school children between the ages of 9 and 12 years. It concentrates on the wider application of calculator skills as tools of investigation and problem solving, with a particular emphasis on work on decimals and the associated concepts. Work on the calculator memory and some of the general functions of a calculator are also included.

Each book has been closely related to the content of mainstream mathematics schemes. However, the provision of materials also takes account of the fact that children using calculators, once they are familiar with the basic operations, are able to work at a slightly higher arithmetical level than the mainstream schemes would seem to suggest. Each of the books, therefore, concentrates on the *processes* of arithmetical and mathematical thinking and activity rather than on purely numerical manipulation. This reflects directly the *National Curriculum Proposals* which, in paragraph 3.33 state: 'Using a calculator effectively depends on an understanding of the number operations to be performed on the calculator, an estimate of the expected answer, a correct sequence of operations on the keyboard, and an intelligent interpretation of the results.' All these aspects are included in *Calculated to Please*.

Using *Calculated to Please*

In all three books, each of the photocopyable sheets for the children is linked to a page of teachers' notes. Together, these teachers' pages form a comprehensive set of notes designed to:

- help teachers to see the purpose of each activity;
- indicate clearly the level of mathematical skill required of the child;
- suggest additional equipment which is essential, or at least useful, to each activity;
- indicate ways in which each page might be used with a group or individual;
- suggest, where appropriate, further activities, discussion or extensions to the work done.
- provide answers to the questions on the children's pages or indicate likely solutions;

A single class contains children with a wide range of aptitudes, abilities and attitudes and the material can be used flexibly to match these various needs. The single-page format allows individuals or groups to work at different levels and on different topics, according to the wishes of the teacher.

Why do you need *Calculated to Please?*

Your school probably has a single commercially produced scheme, or a school-based scheme which integrates several published resources. Such schemes vary considerably in quality and provision of materials and few have made a serious effort to provide suitable calculator activities for children. Similarly, few have made a serious effort to provide materials which can be used to match children's individual needs.

Calculated to Please has been written to provide a flexible resource for busy teachers. It can be

integrated with a mainstream scheme if desired, or retained as the basis of a calculator course for children. Ideally it would be used to provide children with extra general motivational activities, which themselves develop some of the more important mental resources to enable children to deal more effectively with their current and future mathematical learning. Thus a measure of integration, combined with specific use as a topic on 'calculators', would seem to be the best mode of working with the materials.

Choosing a calculator

There is a vast range of calculators on the market, many of which are suitable for use in primary classrooms. Many children possess their own calculators which should be examined carefully to assess their suitability for primary-school use. It would be useful to check with the Local Education Authority before making a bulk purchase of calculators for a school.

One aspect of choice which can be of particular importance is that of the 'logic' of the calculator, that is, its ability to operate on the numbers in the order in which they are entered into the calculator by the user. There is a clear choice to be made in the mode of operation of the calculator. Two types are available.

Arithmetic logic will produce the following:

| 3 | + | 4 | × | 5 | = | 35. |

That is, the calculation is carried out in the order of entry of the numbers and operations.

Algebraic logic will produce the following:

| 3 | + | 4 | × | 5 | = | 23. |

That is, the calculation gives priority to the operations of multiplication (and division). This is *algebraically* correct, but can cause problems for younger children who have not met the use of brackets. However, such a calculator will conform to the 'order of entry' mode if the user presses:

| 3 | + | 4 | = | × | 5 | = | 35. |

That is, the equals key is pressed to 'lock in' the first part of the calculation before proceeding. Alternatively, the memory can be used to the same effect.

Most primary school calculators use arithmetic logic. All advanced or scientific calculators use algebraic logic.

Assessment of progress

Because a calculator is purely a tool, and not an end in itself, assessment can be made on a more flexible basis than is the case with the mainstream mathematics curriculum. Use of a calculator is not amenable to formal testing, but is part of the general process of mathematical activity.

Assessment should therefore be *formative*, that is to say, it should be concerned with how well the child is learning. The aims of assessment in this area should be:

- to help children to see what you expect of them;
- to help you, as the teacher, to use the materials of the 'course' more effectively;
- to allow useful interaction between teacher and child;
- to encourage children to respond positively and creatively to calculators in the classroom;
- to provide rapid feedback to the child about progress;
- to allow you to diagnose weakness.

To aid the assessment and record keeping of children's progress in calculator use, a checklist of selected items of appropriate knowledge, skills and attitudes is included in this book on the next six pages. The fifty items on the checklist are not meant to be an exhaustive survey, but rather to indicate the range and sequence of development in a child's ability to use, and his or her degree of acceptance of, calculators as a major force in present and future mathematical learning.

It should be noted that items 41 to 50 require a judgement from you about the degree of 'appropriateness' of children's responses. They are general aspects of calculator use which can be considered at all levels of work. They are subdivisions of what was referred to in the HMI/DES document *Mathematics 5–16* as 'the sensible use of a calculator'.

A sequence of content and skill objectives related to calculator use

Name _____

Class _____

1 Experience and use of the ON/OFF switch.

2 Experience of the calculator display numerals.

3 Experience of the calculator keyboard numerals.

4 Matching of the keyboard numerals and calculator display numerals.

5 Matching of printed, handwritten, keyboard and display numerals.

6 Experience of the operation keys of addition and subtraction.

7 Experience of the 'equals' key.

8 Recognition and use of $\boxed{C}$, $\boxed{CE}$ or $\boxed{C/CE}$ keys to clear the calculator and display.

9 Use of the calculator to create and check one-step addition bonds;
   (a) to 10   E.g. $\boxed{C}\boxed{3}\boxed{+}\boxed{4}\boxed{=}$ $\boxed{\qquad\qquad\qquad 7.}$
   (b) to 20.

A sequence of content and skill objectives related to calculator use

Name _____

Class _____

10 Use of the calculator to create and check two-step addition bonds;
    (a) to 10   E.g. [C] [1] [+] [2] [+] [3] [=] [_____ 6.]
    (b) to 20.

11 Use of the calculator to create and check one-step subtraction bonds;
    (a) to 10   (b) to 20.

12 Given an unfinished equation, to choose the operation key [+] or [−] to create a display number less than 20.

13 Extension of addition and subtraction calculator skills to numbers less than 100, through puzzles and investigations.

14 Use of a calculator to check and illustrate the inverse nature of the processes of addition and subtraction.

15 Experience and use of the constant function of the calculator.

16 Experience of multiplication as repeated addition, using a calculator to illustrate the process.

A sequence of content and skill objectives related to calculator use

Name _____

Class _____

17 Use of the calculator to create and check multiplication bonds.

18 Experience of division as repeated subtraction, using a calculator to illustrate the process.

19 Use of a calculator in simple chain calculations involving combinations of the four operations of addition, subtraction, multiplication and division.

20 Appropriate use of a calculator to check simple estimation skills based on rounding numbers.

21 Use of a calculator to create 'upside-down' words as a reinforcement of keyboard skills.

22 Use of a calculator to *continue* a given number pattern or sequence.

23 Use of a calculator to *complete* a given number pattern or sequence by finding the missing numbers.

24 Use of a calculator to *create* simple number patterns.

A sequence of content and skill objectives related to calculator use

Name _____

Class _____

25 Experience of the decimal point on the calculator.

26 Use of the calculator in 'decimal' place value situations.

27 Use of a calculator in money computations.

28 Use of a calculator in length computations.

29 Use of a calculator in area computations.

30 Use of a calculator in mass computations.

31 Use of a calculator in volume and capacity computations.

32 Use of a calculator in time and speed computations.

33 Use of the calculator memory keys in chain computations.

34 Use of a calculator in ordering fractions.

A sequence of content and skill objectives related to calculator use

Name _____

Class _____

35 Use of a calculator in matching fractions and decimals.

36 Recognition and use of the $\boxed{\%}$ key.

37 Recognition and use of the $\boxed{+/-}$ key.

38 Recognition and use of the $\boxed{x^2}$ key.

39 Recognition and use of the $\boxed{\sqrt{}}$ key.

40 Recognition and use of the $\boxed{1/x}$ key.

The following are more general aspects of calculator experience and use, which can be considered at all levels of children's work.

41 Appropriate use of the calculator for checking answers or estimates.

42 Appropriate use of the calculator to generate a large number of examples to aid generalisation of rules.

A sequence of content and skill objectives related to calculator use

Name _____

Class _____

43 Appropriate use of the calculator to reduce the burden of calculation when using large numbers.

44 Appropriate use of the calculator to play games specifically designed for calculator involvement.

45 Appropriate use of a calculator to play general number games.

46 Appropriate observation and discussion of 'new' concepts arising from calculator use, e.g. negative numbers.

47 Appropriate use of the calculator in the application of mathematics to the environment.

48 Appropriate use of the calculator in mathematical investigations.

49 Appropriate use of calculators across the curriculum, e.g. in science, history, geography and environmental/ social studies.

50 Development of a sensible attitude to the existence, use and potential of calculators in school work and in everyday life.

Treasure trail ①

● ● ● ● ● ●

Activity/Purpose

The purpose of the activity is to develop the child's understanding that 'tables' are created by addition of numbers of equal size; and to introduce (or remind the child about) the constant function of the calculator.

Two 'routes' are found and coloured on the grid, the green route following an 'add 4' sequence and the red route following an 'add 6' sequence. The crossing point is found and named.

Previous mathematical knowledge and skill required

Knowledge of the table of 4s and the table of 6s.

Notes on using the page

Remind the child of the clues, as stated on the page. If the child has previous experience of the constant functions for addition and subtraction, these can be used to find the routes quickly. Suitable experiences are to be found in *Calculated to Please Books 1 and 2*.

If the child has no previous experience of the constant functions, allow the longer manual method to be used, combined with mentally 'counting on'. When the exercise is understood, the use of the constant functions can be explained, i.e.:

to add 4, press ⁴ ⁺ ⁺ ⁼ ⁰ ⁴ ⁼ ⁼ ...
to add 6, press ⁶ ⁺ ⁺ ⁼ ⁰ ⁶ ⁼ ⁼ ...

● ● ● ● ● ●

 Calculator.

 Green and red coloured pencils or felt-tip pens.

Answers/Solutions

The 'add 4' route   4 8 12 16 20 24 28 32 36 40 44 48 52 56 60 64 68 72 76 80 84 88 92.

The 'add 6' route   6 12 18 24 30 36 42 48 54 60 66 72 78 84 90 96.

Although the multiples of 4 and 6 coincide at many numbers, the *routes* cross only at the 60 square.

Encourage the children to retrace the route by subtracting four or six from the 'treasure' square. It is important for the child to be able to see the inverse nature of addition and subtraction.

○ Ⓝ Ⓞ Ⓣ Ⓔ Ⓢ

Links with our own maths scheme

Other activities and extensions used

General evaluation of the children's work

Treasure trail

There are **two** secret trails on this grid.
Use these clues to find, **colour** and follow them.

Clues
1. The **green** route follows a line of 'add 4'.
2. The **red** route follows a line of 'add 6'.
3. You can only move up left ← or right →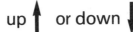

   up ↑ or down ↓ .
4. The two routes cross on **one** square.
5. Use your calculator to help you.

46	42	44	48	52	60	64	88	96
38	36	40	58	56	72	78	84	90
34	32	62	54	60	66	70	74	86
30	28	24	48	64	68	72	76	80
14	22	20	42	36	48	54	82	84
8	12	16	24	30	34	48	84	88
Start 4	Start 6	12	18	24	32	72	76	92

These two routes cross on square [ ]

PUZZLE: ADDING CONSTANTS TO CREATE 'TABLES'.

Mix and match ②

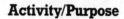

Activity/Purpose

The purpose of the activity is to encourage the child to use the calculator to check which of the possible combinations of given digits will produce a given target answer.

Using one or more mental, written or calculator methods, the child combines the given digits with +, −, ×, or ÷. Various answers emerge, only one of which is the target number. This is recorded on the five blank calculator keys provided.

Previous mathematical knowledge and skill required

Experience of the four rules of number.

Notes on using the page

Briefly discuss the worked example. Stress that **all three** digits must be used and that the **order** of the digits will need to be changed.
Discuss the fact that different pairs of operation keys are used in each item and that the order of the operations is important, as is the order of the digits.
Allow 'working' by any method, but insist on a final check using the calculator before recording.

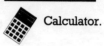

EQUIPMENT

Calculator.

ADDITIONAL ACTIVITIES EXTENSIONS

Encourage the child to investigate:
(a) Other 'answers' which emerge from the use of 3 digits. Note that a systematic approach is essential, i.e. given a fixed order of numbers, combine them using (+ +), (+ −), (+ ×), (+ ÷), (− +), (− −), (− ×), (− ÷), and so on.
(b) Other sets of 3 digits which give specified 'answers', e.g. $11=6+2+3$ or $5+4+2$, and so on.

Answers/Solutions

$6+5\times1=11$	$8\times6\div3=16$
$8+9-5=12$	$4\times5-3=17$
$7\times3-8=13$	$8\div4\times9=18$
$6\times3-4=14$	$9\times2+1=19$
$5\times9\div3=15$	$7-3\times5=20$

Links with our own maths scheme

Other activities and extensions used

General evaluation of the children's work

Mix and match

Use **all three** numbers to make each target display number.
You choose the **order** of the numbers and the **signs**.

Use your calculator to check **before** recording!

Use	Target display	How?
① ⑤ ⑥	11.	6 + 5 × 1 =
⑤ ⑧ ⑨	12.	
⑧ ③ ⑦	13.	
③ ④ ⑥	14.	
③ ⑤ ⑨	15.	
③ ⑥ ⑧	16.	
③ ④ ⑤	17.	
④ ⑧ ⑨	18.	
⑨ ① ②	19.	
③ ⑦ ⑤	20.	

Name _____   Class _____

USING A CALULATOR FOR RAPID CHECKING OF NUMBER SENTENCES.

© Unwin Hyman
Calculated to Please 3

Enders 1 and 2 ③–④

INVESTIGATION OF LAST-DIGIT MULTIPLICATION PATTERNS, USING THE CONSTANT FUNCTION

Activity/Purpose

The activity is an investigation of the patterns which emerge when recording the **last digits** of inputs and outputs, when multiplying given numbers. The child sets the constant function of the calculator and uses it for rapid multiplication of a given set of numbers by the constant. The end digits (enders) are recorded on a ladder.

Previous mathematical knowledge and skill required

Understanding of the term 'digit'.
Familiarity with multiplication tables 2 to 10, inclusive.

Notes on using the pages

Ensure that the child is familiar with the constant function of the calculator from previous pages of *Calculated to Please*. With the less able child, discussion of the introductory example would provide additional security for success.

The first page can be used alone, and the second used only for a child able to develop the investigation. Ensure that the **points** are joined using **straight** lines to allow the pattern to be clearly seen.

Answers/Solutions

See below.

EQUIPMENT

 Calculator.

 Ruler.

ADDITIONAL ACTIVITIES EXTENSIONS

1. When the activity is completed, discuss whether the pattern works for **all** inputs.

2. Discuss the 'shape' and design of the ladders to find items of consistency, e.g. (a) on the ×5 ladder all answers end in 0 or 5; (b) on the ×2 ladder all answers are even.

3. Relate the work to the tests of divisibility considered in *Calculated to Please Book 2*.

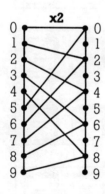

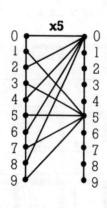

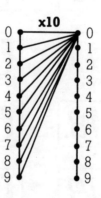

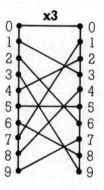

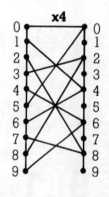

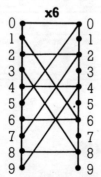

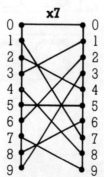

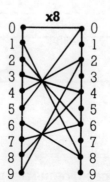

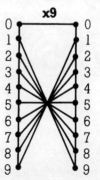

Enders 1

Input numbers

260	82	514	76	38
151	253	135	127	19

Set your calculator for **multiply by 2** like this: 2 × × = 0

1. Choose an input number.
2. Use the calculator to multiply it by 2.
3. Join the **last digit** of the input number to the **last digit** of the answer.

Finish this (×2) ladder.

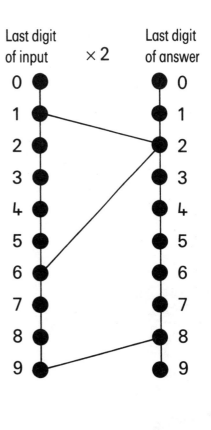

Last digit of input   × 2   Last digit of answer

Now do these ladders in the same way.

5 × × = 0

Last digit of input   × 5   Last digit of answer

1 0 × × = 0

Last digit of input   × 10   Last digit of answer

3 × × = 0

Last digit of input   × 3   Last digit of answer

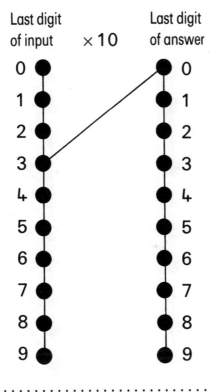

Name _____   Class _____

INVESTIGATION OF LAST-DIGIT MULTIPLICATION PATTERNS USING
A CALCULATOR CONSTANT FOR MULTIPLICATION.

© Unwin Hyman
Calculated to Please 3

Enders 2

④

Input numbers

260
151
82
253
514
135
76
127
38
19

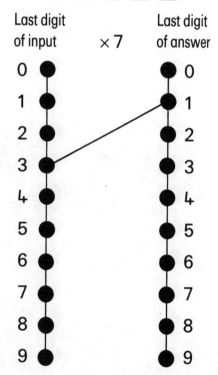

$4 \times \times = 0$

Last digit of input	$\times 4$	Last digit of answer
0		0
1		1
2		2
3		3
4		4
5		5
6		6
7		7
8		8
9		9

$6 \times \times = 0$

Last digit of input	$\times 6$	Last digit of answer
0		0
1		1
2		2
3		3
4		4
5		5
6		6
7		7
8		8
9		9

$7 \times \times = 0$

Last digit of input	$\times 7$	Last digit of answer
0		0
1		1
2		2
3		3
4		4
5		5
6		6
7		7
8		8
9		9

$8 \times \times = 0$

Last digit of input	$\times 8$	Last digit of answer
0		0
1		1
2		2
3		3
4		4
5		5
6		6
7		7
8		8
9		9

$9 \times \times = 0$

Last digit of input	$\times 9$	Last digit of answer
0		0
1		1
2		2
3		3
4		4
5		5
6		6
7		7
8		8
9		9

Name _____

Class _____

INVESTIGATION OF LAST-DIGIT MULTIPLICATION PATTERNS USING
A CALCULATOR CONSTANT FOR MULTIPLICATION.

Teens: Adding and subtracting

● ● ● ● ●

Activity/Purpose

The purpose of the activity is to use the constant function of the calculator to develop the child's skills in estimating.

The child sets the calculator for the given constant. Then, given a starting number and a target or finishing number, he or she **estimates** how many 'jumps' of the given size are needed from the start to reach the target. The estimate is recorded by ringing the display in which the child thinks the target will appear. The constant function is then used to create and record the sequence, and the child is asked to decide whether or not he or she made a good estimate.

Previous mathematical knowledge and skill required

Experience of addition and subtraction of hundreds, tens and units.
Familiarity with the constant functions for addition and subtraction.

Notes on using the pages

Remind the child of the technique for setting up and using the constant function of the calculator. Emphasise that the good guess or estimate must be made **first**, before creating the sequence using the constant. If necessary work through the first example with the child.
For the less able child it may be useful to use the unnumbered blank of the sheet, at the back of the book, to employ smaller numbers with a smaller constant.

● ● ● ● ●

Answers/Solutions

Adding teens								
2.	13	29	45	61	77	93	109	
3.	19	35	51	67	83	99		
4.	24	40	56	72	88			
5.	32	48	64	80	96	112	128	
6.	47	63	79	95	111			
7.	55	71	87	103	119	1³5	151	167

Subtracting								
2.	106	93	80	67	54	41	28	15
3.	100	87	74	61	48	35	22	
4.	81	68	55	42	29			
5.	99	86	73	60	47	34		
6.	124	111	98	85	72	59	46	
7.	157	144	131	118	105	92	79	66	53

EQUIPMENT

 Calculator.

**ADDITIONAL ACTIVITIES
EXTENSIONS**

1. Use the unnumbered blank of this page, at the back of the book, to work to other targets from other starting points using other 'teen' steps, in both addition and subtraction.

2. Discuss the method used by the child to decide on the likely location of the *finish* number, e.g. rounding.

Adding teens

Set your calculator to **add 16** like this: [1][6][+][+][=][0]

How many 16s must you add to get from **Start** to **Finish**?

First make a **good guess** and ring the display where you think the **Finish** will be.

Then fill in all the displays between the **Start** and **Finish** numbers, counting in 16s.

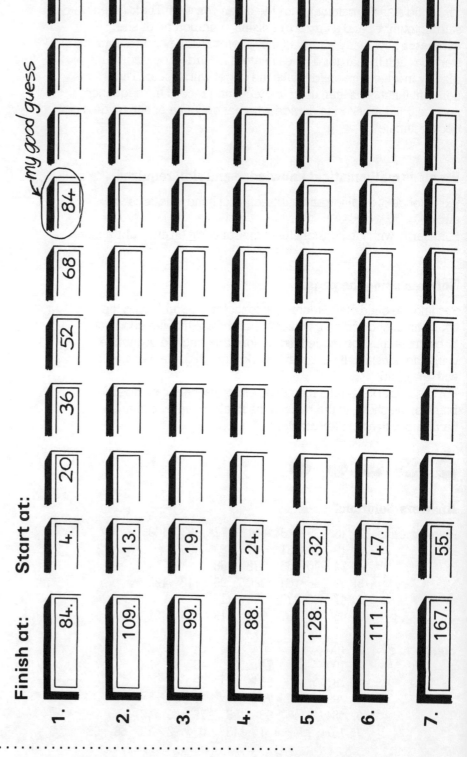

Good guess?

my good guess → 84 *yes!*

Start at:

Finish at:

	Start at:				84		Finish at:
1.	4.	20	36	52	68		84.
2.	13.						109.
3.	19.						99.
4.	24.						88.
5.	32.						128.
6.	47.						111.
7.	55.						167.

Name _____

Class _____

© Unwin Hyman
Calculated to Please 3

Subtracting teens

● ● ● ● ● ● ●

Set your calculator to **subtract 13** like this: 1 3 − = 0

How many 13s must you subtract to get from **Start** to **Finish**?

First make a **good guess** and ring the display where you **think** the **Finish** will be.

Then fill in all the displays between the **Start** and **Finish** numbers, counting back in 13s.

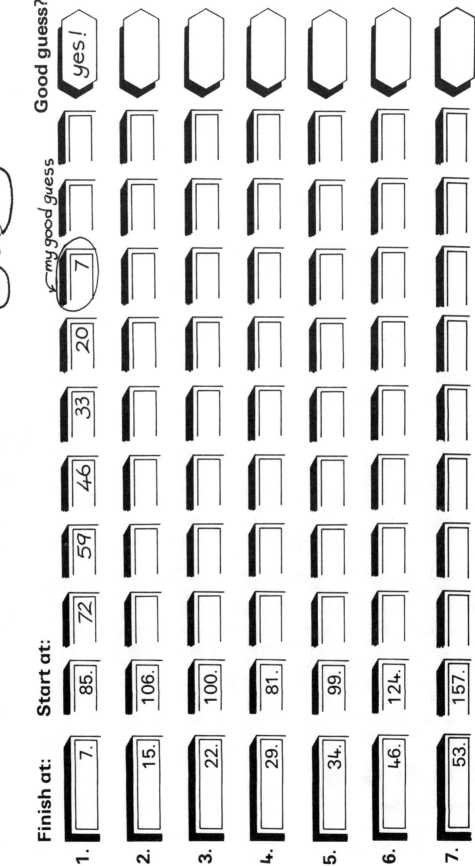

Good guess? yes!

my good guess

Finish at: **Start at:**

	Finish at:	Start at:							my good guess				Good guess?
1.	7.	85.	72	59	46	33	20	7				yes!
2.	15.	106.										
3.	22.	100.										
4.	29.	81.										
5.	34.	99.										
6.	46.	124.										
7.	53.	157.										

Name _____ Class _____

USING THE CALCULATOR CONSTANT FUNCTION TO DEVELOP ESTIMATION SKILL.

© Unwin Hyman
Calculated to Please 3

Cash in/Cash out ⑦-⑨

Activity/Purpose

The use and 'reading' of a calculator for making and checking money calculations is an important social and mathematical skill. The activities on these pages reinforce the child's ability to read and write money notation and to use the calculator for the four rules in relation to money.

Cash in concentrates on keying in and reading amounts of money, matching words, symbols, the key sequence and the display.

Cash out presents examples of money calculations to help children to learn the sequences of keys, and the associated displays, which produce given totals, differences, products or quotients. Then the children apply the knowledge they have gained.

Previous mathematical knowledge and skill required

Experience of money calculations in written *and* practical contexts.
Ability to link amounts of money written as pounds, or pence, or both.

Notes on using the pages

It is recommended that the pages are dealt with in the order in which they appear. Children should be encouraged to use real or token coins where appropriate to check the calculator answers.

Stress the need always to **write** money amounts with **two** places of decimals.
Discuss the alternative ways to input, say, 50p, i.e. 0·50 or 0·5 or ·5. Continue to remind children that C/CE should always be pressed between 'whole' calculations, to clear previous entries.

Most errors arise because the child enters the pence incorrectly, either forgetting the decimal point or entering 3p as 0·3 instead of 0·03. The child should be encouraged to check each display to see whether or not the answer is reasonable, thus reinforcing the skill of estimation.

In all calculations it is advisable to encourage estimation or 'good guessing' of the answer **before** using the calculator.

EQUIPMENT

 Calculator.

 Real or token coins.

ADDITIONAL ACTIVITIES EXTENSIONS

1. Discussion of the sequence of displays can be fruitful, e.g. numbers that are keyed in always appear as identical numbers, but the input of signs changes the display. Interestingly, = produces an identical response to the sign pressed previously.

2. Encourage use of the calculator to check answers in your mainstream mathematics scheme.

3. Encourage reversal of the processes, i.e. check subtraction by adding; division by multiplication; multiplication by division.

Answers/Solutions

Cash in   3p → 0.03
       30p → 0.3 or 0.30
       Three pounds three pence → 3.03
       Thirty-three pence → 0.33
       £3 → 3.
       £30 → 30.
       £33 → 33.
       Three pounds thirty pence 3.3 or 3.30

Cash out

Addition
1. £2·93 **2.** £6·15 **3.** £1·75

Subtraction
1. £2·45 **2.** £4·24 **3.** £8·39

Multiplication
1. £7·76 **2.** £1·68 **3.** £18·87 **4.** £12·51

Division
1. £0·84 or 84p
2. £0·80 (*not* £0·8) or 80p
3. £0·06 or 6p
4. £0·95 or 95p

● ● ● ● ● ● ●

There are special ways to key in amounts of **money**.
Fill in the displays for these amounts.

Words	Amount	Press	Display
Five pounds	£5	⑤ ▶	5.
Two pounds fifteen pence	£2·15	② · ① ⑤ ▶	
One pound fifty pence	£1·50	① · ⑤ ⓪ ▶	
	or	① · ⑤ ▶	
Eight pounds two pence	£8·02	⑧ · ⓪ ② ▶	
Seventy-five pence	£0·75	· ⑦ ⑤ ▶	
Four pence	£0·04	· ⓪ ④ ▶	

Match and **join** the amounts and displays.

3p

0.33

3.03

3.3

Three pounds three pence

£30

Three pounds thirty pence

Thirty-three pence

0.3

£3

3.

30p

33.

30.

£33

0.03

....

Name _____   Class _____

ENTERING AMOUNTS OF MONEY INTO A CALCULATOR.

© Unwin Hyman
Calculated to Please 3

Cash out 1

Addition of money

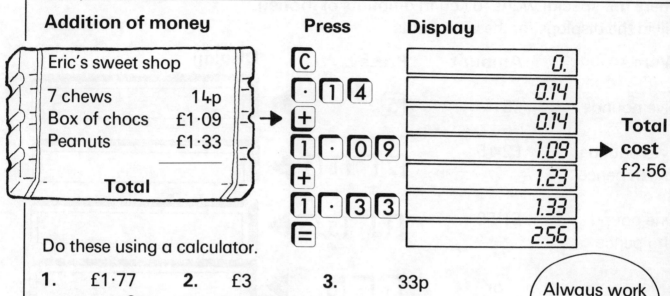

Eric's sweet shop

7 chews	14p
Box of chocs	£1·09
Peanuts	£1·33
Total	

Press

Press	Display
C	0.
· 1 4	0.14
+	0.14
1 · 0 9	1.09
+	1.23
1 · 3 3	1.33
=	2.56

Total cost £2·56

Do these using a calculator.

1.
```
   £1·77
      3p
     10p
  +£1·03
  _____
      £
```

2.
```
     £3
      7p
     99p
  +£2·09
  _____
      £
```

3.
```
      33p
      49p
       7p
  +    86p
  _____
       £
```

Always work in pounds!

Subtraction of money

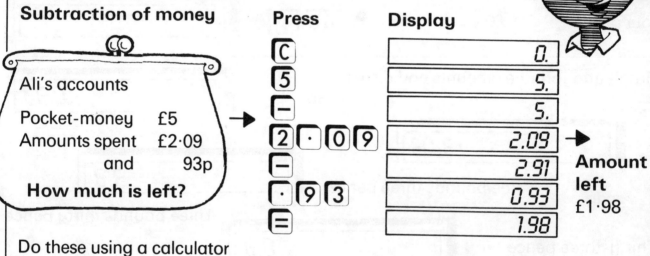

Ali's accounts

Pocket-money   £5
Amounts spent   £2·09
          and   93p

How much is left?

Press	Display
C	0.
5	5.
−	5.
2 · 0 9	2.09
−	2.91
· 9 3	0.93
=	1.98

Amount left £1·98

Do these using a calculator

1. £4 pocket money.
Amounts spent   50p
          and   £1·05

Amount left £ _____

2.
```
   £6·01
  −£1·77
  _____
      £
```

3. £10 birthday gift.
Amounts spent:
£1, 50p, 10p and 1p.

Amount left £ _____

Name _____   Class _____

CALCULATOR ADDITION AND SUBTRACTION OF MONEY.

Cash out 2

Multiplication of money

On holiday you spend 75p each day on sweets. The holiday lasts for 7 days. **How much altogether** do you spend on sweets?

Press	Display
C	0.
. 7 5	0.75
x	0.75
7	7.
=	5.25

→ **Total spent £5·25**

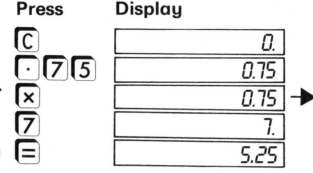

Do these on your calculator.

1. 97p × 8 = £ ____

2. 6 × £0·28 = £ ____

3. 17p × 111 = £ ____

4. £1·39 × 9 = £ ____

Always work in pounds!

Division of money

Share £6·16 equally between 8 people. **How much does each person get?**

Press	Display
C	0.
6 . 1 6	6.16
÷	6.16
8	8.
=	0.77

→ **Each person gets £0·77 or 77p**

Do these on your calculator.

1. £7·56 ÷ 9 = £ ____ or ____ p

2. £4 ÷ 5 = £ ____ or ____ p

3. £9 ÷ 150 = £ ____ or ____ p

4. £17·10 ÷ 18 = £ ____ or ____ p

Name _____ Class _____

CALCULATOR MULTIPLICATION AND DIVISION OF MONEY.

© Unwin Hyman
Calculated to Please 3

Following numbers 1, 2, 3 and 4

Activity/Purpose

The purpose of the activity is to investigate aspects of **consecutive numbers,** using a calculator and other computational methods. Use of a calculator is recommended for all but the simplest items because of the speed with which hypotheses can be tested, using a range of numbers.

Previous mathematical knowledge and skill required

Experience of the concepts and algorithms of the four rules of number, using tens and units.
Experience of the simple tests of divisibility (see *Calculated to Please Book 2*).

Notes on using the pages

Ensure that the child understands the term 'consecutive numbers' before attempting the activity.
It is essential that the pages are dealt with in the order in which they appear, so that the principle of each can be used to enhance learning in the following pages.
Where appropriate a worked example is shown. This should be briefly discussed and checked before the child works alone on the activity.

Links with our own maths scheme

Other activities and extensions used

General evaluation of the children's work

● ● ● ● ●

Answers/Solutions

Sheet 1: Adding consecutive numbers

14+15= 29	23+24= 47
26+27= 53	39+40= 79
41+42= 83	98+99=197
51+52=103	86+87=173
78+79=157	45+46= 91
93+94=187	57+58=115
62+63=125	82+83=165

Sheet 2: Multiplying consecutive numbers

10×11=110	14×15=210
19×20=380	25×26=650
11×12=132	22×23=506
18×19=342	28×29=812
17×18=306	12×13=156
31×32=992	21×22=462
16×17=272	13×14=182

Sheet 3

1, 2, 4, 8 and 16 **cannot** be made from additions of consecutive numbers.

3=1+2
5=2+3
6=1+2+3
7=3+4
9=4+5 or 2+3+4
10=1+2+3+4
11=5+6
12=3+4+5
13=6+7
14=2+3+4+5
15=7+8 or 1+2+3+4+5 or 4+5+6
17=8+9
18=3+4+5+6 or 5+6+7
19=9+10
20=2+3+4+5+6

The missing key is $\boxed{2}$. This, used in the given key sequence, produces the series 1, 2, 4, 8, 16.

Sheet 4

A The answers (product of 2 consecutive numbers) are always divisible by 2.

B The answers (product of 3 consecutive numbers) are always divisible by 3.

C The answers (product of 4 consecutive numbers) are always divisible by 4.

ADDITIONAL ACTIVITIES EXTENSIONS

1. Discuss the fact that:
   (a) Adding consecutive numbers (O+E) or (E+O) always produces an **odd** number in the display. Does this always apply?
   (b) Multiplying consecutive numbers (O×E) or (E×O) always produces an even number in the display. Does this always apply?

2. There are short cuts that can be used to find the consecutive numbers on sheets 1 and 2. Discuss them *after* the pages have been completed! With addition of consecutive numbers, halve the display number and the 'whole number' part of the answer tells you the first consecutive number. With multiplication of consecutive numbers, the first number can be found by finding the square root of the display (assuming a square-root key is available). The 'whole number' part of the answer is the first consecutive number.

3. On sheet 3, numbers greater than 20 can be investigated in the same way. All except **32, 64,** etc. can be formed from consecutive numbers.

4. On sheet 4, encourage the child to investigate products of five, six, seven, . . . consecutive numbers. The pattern of divisibility continues to apply.

5. Make an unnumbered blank of this activity and use it to investigate other sums and products of consecutive numbers.

Numbers which follow on, like 3 and 4, or 18 and 19,
or 103 and 104, are called **consecutive numbers**.
They are 'next door neighbours' on a number line.

Fill in the **consecutive numbers** that give the display number.

[1][4][+][1][5][=] 29.

[ ][ ][+][ ][ ][=] 47.

[ ][ ][+][ ][ ][=] 53.

[ ][ ][+][ ][ ][=] 79.

[ ][ ][+][ ][ ][=] 83.

[ ][ ][+][ ][ ][=] 197.

[ ][ ][+][ ][ ][=] 103.

[ ][ ][+][ ][ ][=] 173.

[ ][ ][+][ ][ ][=] 157.

[ ][ ][+][ ][ ][=] 91.

[ ][ ][+][ ][ ][=] 187.

[ ][ ][+][ ][ ][=] 115.

[ ][ ][+][ ][ ][=] 125.

[ ][ ][+][ ][ ][=] 165.

Name _____   Class _____

CALCULATOR INVESTIGATION OF CONSECUTIVE NUMBERS.

© Unwin Hyman
Calculated to Please 3

Following numbers 2

Numbers which follow on, like 3 and 4, or 18 and 19,
or 103 and 104, are called **consecutive numbers**.

Fill in the **consecutive numbers** that give the display number.

| 1 | 0 | × | 1 | 1 | = | 110. |

| ☐ | ☐ | × | ☐ | ☐ | = | 210. |

| ☐ | ☐ | × | ☐ | ☐ | = | 380. |

| ☐ | ☐ | × | ☐ | ☐ | = | 650. |

| ☐ | ☐ | × | ☐ | ☐ | = | 132. |

| ☐ | ☐ | × | ☐ | ☐ | = | 506. |

| ☐ | ☐ | × | ☐ | ☐ | = | 342. |

| ☐ | ☐ | × | ☐ | ☐ | = | 812. |

| ☐ | ☐ | × | ☐ | ☐ | = | 306. |

| ☐ | ☐ | × | ☐ | ☐ | = | 156. |

| ☐ | ☐ | × | ☐ | ☐ | = | 992. |

| ☐ | ☐ | × | ☐ | ☐ | = | 462. |

| ☐ | ☐ | × | ☐ | ☐ | = | 272. |

| ☐ | ☐ | × | ☐ | ☐ | = | 182. |

Name _____ Class _____

CALCULATOR INVESTIGATION OF CONSECUTIVE NUMBERS.

© Unwin Hyman
Calculated to Please 3

Following numbers 3

Numbers which follow on, like 3 and 4, or 5 and 6 and 7, are called **consecutive numbers**.

Investigate which of these numbers can be written as **the sum of two or more consecutive numbers**.

1	no
2	no
3	1 + 2 = 3
4	
5	
6	
7	
8	
9	
10	
11	5 + 6 = 11
12	
13	
14	
15	
16	
17	
18	
19	
20	

Some have been done for you!

=11

2 different ways.

+6

3 different ways.

5

2 different ways.

Which **number key** should you put in this sequence of keys to show you the numbers you could **not** do on this page?

Which number key? → ☐ ✕ ✕ ═ 0 1 ═ ═ ═ ═

....

Name _____   Class _____

CALCULATOR INVESTIGATION OF CONSECUTIVE NUMBERS.

© Unwin Hyman
Calculated to Please 3

Following numbers 4

Numbers which follow on, like 3 and 4, or 5 and 6 and 7, are called **consecutive numbers**.

A Two consecutive numbers

Multiply these **2** consecutive numbers.

6 × 7 =

7 × 8 =

17 × 18 =

23 × 24 =

Do some more of your own on the back of the sheet.

These answers are always exactly divisible by ☐

B Three consecutive numbers

Multiply these **3** consecutive numbers.

2 × 3 × 4 =

5 × 6 × 7 =

8 × 9 × 10 =

11 × 12 × 13 =

Do some more of your own on the back of the sheet.

These answers are always exactly divisible by ☐

C Four consecutive numbers

Multiply these **4** consecutive numbers.

2 × 3 × 4 × 5 =

3 × 4 × 5 × 6 =

4 × 5 × 6 × 7 =

5 × 6 × 7 × 8 =

Do some more of your own on the back of the sheet.

These answers are always exactly divisible by ☐

Name _____ Class _____

CALCULATOR INVESTIGATION OF CONSECUTIVE NUMBERS.

© Unwin Hyman
Calculated to Please 3

Talking calculators ⑭

● ● ● ● ● ●

Activity/Purpose

The purpose is systematically to search for display numbers which appear as 'words' when the calculator is inverted. Note that an unnumbered 'blank' of the sheet is supplied at the back of the book for recording 'words' with initial letters other than B.

Previous mathematical knowledge and skill required

Knowledge of basic number manipulations using the four rules of number.
An open-ended investigation may produce calculations which use the function keys x^2 $\sqrt{x}$ $\frac{1}{x}$ $\%$ $+/-$ but this is unnecessary.

Notes on using the page

Book 2 includes an easier activity using such 'words'.
Allow both calculator-based and non-calculator based discussion and investigation.

● ● ● ● ● ●

Answers/Solutions

B = 8 **H** = h **O** = 0
E = E **I** = l **S** = 5
G = 9 **L** = L **Z** = 2

A basic list would include these 'words'. There are others, depending on your willingness to include slang.

B: BOG(S) BLESS BIB(S) BEE(S) BIG BILLIE(S) BOB(S) BE BELL(S) BILL(S) BESS BEG(S) BIBLE(S) BOILS(S) BLOB(S) BLISS BOGGLE(S) BOBBLE(S) BOOHOO BOO

E: EGG(S) ELSE ELSIE EEL EH

G: GOOSE GOGGLES GOSH GOBBLE(S) GIGGLE(S) GLOBE(S) GEESE GLEE GOES GIG GO GILL(S) GOLLIES

H: HOE(S) HOSE(S) HELL HOLE(S) HILL(S) HE HISS HOG(S) HIGH HELLO HIS HOB(S) HELOISE HOLLIES

I: IGLOO(S) IS ILL I ISLE

L: LESLIE LOG(S) LESS LEG(S) LIE(S) LOOSE LOSE(S) LOSS LEGLESS LEGO LOLLIES LOOE LOOSISH LOLL LILLIE LEE

O: OH OOZE(S) OBOE(S) OIL(S) OGLE(S) OSLO

S: SIEGE(S) SIGH(S) SIZE(S) SLOB(S) SOLO(S) SLOSH(ES) SOB(S) SOIL(S) S.O.S. SOLE(S) SLOG(S) SHELL(S) SHOE(S) SEE(S) SLEIGH(S) SIEZE(S) SELL(S) SHE SILLIES SO SLOE SILL SOHO

Z: ZOO(S)

EQUIPMENT

 1 or 2 calculators.

ADDITIONAL ACTIVITIES EXTENSIONS

1. Making a crossword puzzle using the words.

2. Writing a story with gaps to be filled by 'words' found through calculations.

3. Making compound words and part-words.

Talking calculators

Work with a friend.
Find as many upside-down 'words' as you can.
For each one, write a calculation that puts the word into the display.
Use this sheet to start you off with words starting with **B**.

Word	Number	Calculation
BILL BILLS	7718	3859 × 2

You can write lists of words, numbers and calculations
for these starting letters.

B E G H I L O S Z

Name _____   Class _____

INVESTIGATING AND RECORDING UPSIDE-DOWN 'WORDS', NUMBERS AND
CALCULATIONS.

© Unwin Hyman
Calculated to Please 3

Ages

Activity/Purpose

The purpose of the activity is to encourage the child to learn and memorise a simple key sequence in order to conduct a 'trick' which finds a person's age and birthday month.

Previous mathematical knowledge and skill required

Understanding of the term 'digit'.
Basic keyboard skills, including display, place value and interpretation.
Experience of using a calculator for the four rules of number.

Notes on using the page

Encourage the child to attempt the activity without prior teaching/discussion.
Ensure that the displays are recorded clearly so that the sequence of displays is evident.
The 'last two digits' may need explanation, particularly if, for example, 08 is shown (to be read as the age of 8 years).

EQUIPMENT

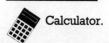 Calculator.

ADDITIONAL ACTIVITIES EXTENSIONS

Encourage the more able child to attempt an explanation of how the 'trick' works, i.e. if M is number of month and A is age in years, the sequence is:

1. M
2. $10 \times M$
3. $10 \times M + 20$
4. $100M + 200$
5. $100M + 165 + 200 = 100M + 365$
6. $100M + 365 + A$
7. $100M + A + 365 - 365 = 100M + A$

In $100M + A$, $100M$ represents the digit in the hundreds column and A represents the digits in the tens and units columns.

 N O T E S

Links with our own maths scheme

Other activities and extensions used

General evaluation of the children's work

Ages

Find a friend's birthday month and age in years by asking them to follow these instructions using a calculator.

Try it here first, using facts about yourself.

1. Key in the **number** of the month of your birthday.

January = 1,   February = 2,   and so on.

Record the displays.

2. Multiply it by 10.   ⊠①⓪🟰

3. Add 20.   ⊞②⓪🟰

4. Multiply by 10.   ⊠①⓪🟰

5. Add 165.   ⊞①⑥⑤🟰

6. Add your age, in years only.   ⊞☐☐🟰

7. Subtract 365.   ⊟③⑥⑤🟰

The **last two** digits tell you the age.

So 11 is 11 years old.
  09 is 9 years old.
  83 is 83 years old!

The **other** digits tell you the birthday month.

So 1 is January
  12 is December.

Try it on a friend, your granny, the dog, ...!

....

Name _____   Class _____

CALCULATOR PUZZLE SEQUENCE REQUIRING MEMORISATION.

Underground numbers ⑯

Activity/Purpose

The purpose of the activity is to use the calculator constant function to create and record a sequence of negative (and positive) numbers on a vertical number line.

The child keys in the constant, followed by the starting number and then a series of $=$ $=$ ... The sequence is observed in the display and recorded as above-ground numbers (positive) and below-ground or underground numbers (negative).

Previous mathematical knowledge and skill required

Experience of number lines and sequences of constant addition and subtraction (the multiplication tables). Experience of the calculator constant function for subtraction.

Notes on using the page

Check first the means by which the calculator **display** shows a negative number. Sometimes it is on the far left and its existence should be pointed out to the child.
Ensure that the minus sign is recorded where appropriate – the oval shape has been included to provide the extra space required.
The child follows the key sequence and records the displays in the order in which they appear.
Encourage estimation or 'good guessing' of the next display *before* the $=$ key is pressed.

Answers/Solutions

1.   4 to −18 in 2s.
2. 10 to −45 in 5s.
3.   6 to −27 in 3s.
4. 12 to −54 in 6s.
5. 18 to −81 in 9s.

○ Ⓝ Ⓞ Ⓣ Ⓔ Ⓢ

EQUIPMENT

Calculator.

ADDITIONAL ACTIVITIES EXTENSIONS

1. Encourage investigation of other constants and starting numbers.

2. Encourage reversal of the process, e.g. in the first example press

   2 $+$ $+$ $=$ 0,
   then $-$ 1 8
   or $+/-$ 1 8
   then $=$ $=$ ...

   If the calculator has a $+/-$ key, this should be used to change the sign on the given starting number.

3. Encourage the child to record positive and negative sequences on a number line, having first created them on the calculator.

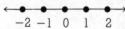
   −2 −1 0 1 2

Underground numbers ⑯

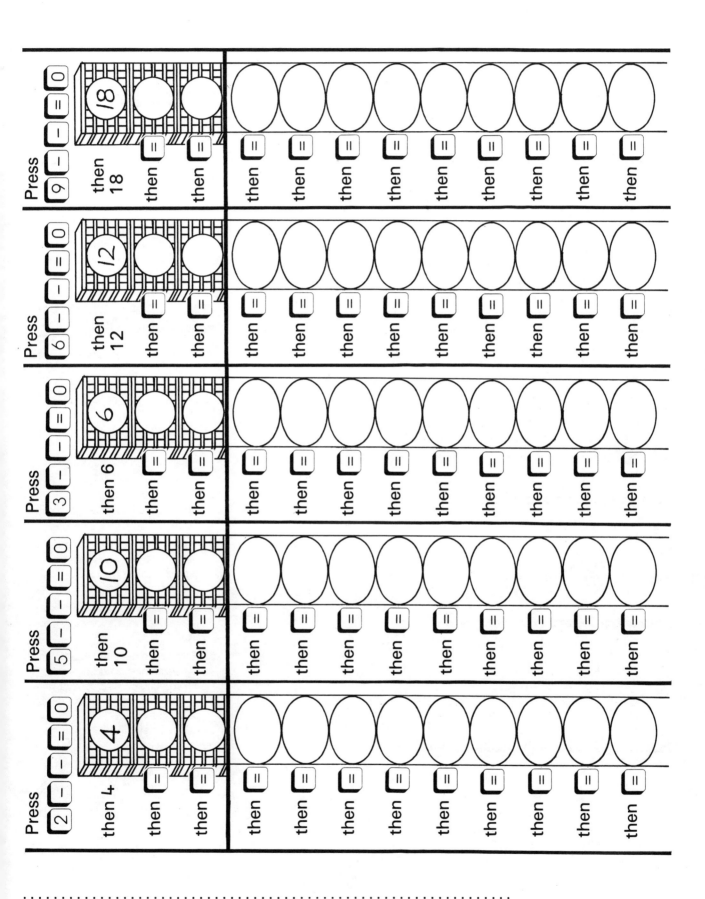

Name _____   Class _____

**USING THE CALCULATOR CONSTANT TO DEVELOP A SEQUENCE OF
NEGATIVE NUMBERS.**

© Unwin Hyman
Calculated to Please 3

Decimal race ⑰

● ● ● ● ● ●

Activity/Purpose

This is a game for two players. The purpose is to develop the child's understanding of the decimal number line in steps of 0·1.

Previous mathematical knowledge and skill required

Experience of decimal place value (one place of decimals only). Familiarity with addition and subtraction of simple decimals.

Notes on using the page

Supply the special dice and briefly check understanding of the rules and the directions to move on the grid.
The important point to make is that the 'score' is interpreted in the way shown on the page, i.e. 0·8 is a move of 8 squares, each of which is 0·1 ($8 \times 0·1 = 0·8$). The calculator can be used as a checking device or as the means of subtraction.

  N O T E S

Links with our own maths scheme

Other activities and extensions used

General evaluation of the children's work

EQUIPMENT

 Calculator.

 Two small counters of different colours.

 Two blank dice or small cubes labelled:
0·1, 0·2, 0·3, 0·4, 0·5, 0·6 and 0·7, 0·8, 0·9, 1·0, 1·1, 1·2

ADDITIONAL ACTIVITIES EXTENSIONS

1. Isolate and discuss the **vertical** patterns/sequences of decimals, e.g.

   column 1: linked by +1·9
   then +0·1
   column 2: linked by +1·7
   then +0·3
   column 3: linked by +1·5
   then +0·5

2. For less able children allow the decimals to be **added**, changing rule 4.

3. Vary the rules. For example allow a player who lands on a whole number to move on to the next whole number.

4. Change the rules so that players move backwards, counting back from 10 to 0·1.

5. Encourage the child to examine the sequence of adding or subtracting 0·1 as a constant. These are created by setting the calculator:
   (a) to add 0·1
   $\boxed{0}\boxed{·}\boxed{1}\boxed{+}\boxed{+}\boxed{=}\boxed{0}$ (start number) $\boxed{=}\boxed{=}$ . . .
   (b) to subtract 0·1
   $\boxed{0}\boxed{·}\boxed{1}\boxed{-}\boxed{-}\boxed{=}\boxed{0}$ (start number) $\boxed{=}\boxed{=}$ . . .

Decimal race

A game for 2 players.

Rules:

1. Choose counters of different colours.
2. Take turns to:

   Throw **both** dice.

   Read the two decimals shown on the dice.

   Subtract the smaller decimal from the larger decimal.

   Move your counter that number of places on the grid.

   For example:  = 0·8,

   so move 8 squares, in steps of 0·1.
3. The first to reach **10** is the winner.

Use your calculator to help you!

Start 0·1	0·2	0·3	0·4	0·5	0·6	0·7	0·8	0·9	1
2	1·9	1·8	1·7	1·6	1·5	1·4	1·3	1·2	1·1
2·1	2·2	2·3	2·4	2·5	2·6	2·7	2·8	2·9	3
4	3·9	3·8	3·7	3·6	3·5	3·4	3·3	3·2	3·1
4·1	4·2	4·3	4·4	4·5	4·6	4·7	4·8	4·9	5
6	5·9	5·8	5·7	5·6	5·5	5·4	5·3	5·2	5·1
6·1	6·2	6·3	6·4	6·5	6·6	6·7	6·8	6·9	7
8	7·9	7·8	7·7	7·6	7·5	7·4	7·3	7·2	7·1
8·1	8·2	8·3	8·4	8·5	8·6	8·7	8·8	8·9	9
10	9·9	9·8	9·7	9·6	9·5	9·4	9·3	9·2	9·1

The winner's name is

....

Name _____

Class _____

> You need
> 1 calculator, 2 small counters, and 2 special dice (ask your teacher for them).

Decimals and fractions 1, 2 and 3 ⑱–⑳

● ● ● ● ● ●

Activity/Purpose

The purpose of the activity is to encourage recognition of equivalent fractions by converting given fractions to decimals and then linking those that are thus shown to be different forms of the same 'number'. The child groups the fraction/decimal equivalents using a colour coding.

Previous mathematical knowledge and skill required

Experience of pictorial and numerical forms of halves, quarters, eighths, fifths, tenths, thirds, sixths and ninths. Simple calculator skills of division and display reading.

Notes on using the pages

It is essential that calculator work on fractions and decimals **follows** practical activities in the recognition and writing of fractions.

Remind the child to clear the calculator between each calculation; and to note that the written decimal form of, say, 0·5 is different to the calculator display form, 0.5, in the position of the decimal point.

It would be useful to have available either the circle form of fraction image:

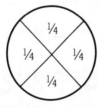

or the strip form , or both.
Ensure that all possible links are made, not just a single pair.

● ● ● ● ● ●

Answers/Solutions

Sheet 1 $\frac{1}{2}=\frac{2}{4}=\frac{4}{8}$

$\frac{1}{4}=\frac{2}{8}$

$\frac{2}{2}=\frac{4}{4}=\frac{8}{8}$

$\frac{3}{4}=\frac{6}{8}$

Sheet 2 $\frac{1}{5}=\frac{2}{10}$

$\frac{3}{5}=\frac{6}{10}$

$\frac{4}{5}=\frac{8}{10}$

$\frac{2}{5}=\frac{4}{10}=\frac{8}{20}$

$\frac{5}{5}=\frac{10}{10}$

Sheet 3 $\frac{1}{3}=\frac{2}{6}=\frac{3}{9}$

$\frac{2}{3}=\frac{4}{6}=\frac{6}{9}$

$\frac{3}{3}=\frac{6}{6}=\frac{9}{9}$

EQUIPMENT

 Calculator.

 Coloured pencils or felt-tip pens.

ADDITIONAL ACTIVITIES EXTENSIONS

1. Encourage the child to write **three more** equivalent fractions for each of the examples given.

2. Discuss the special case of $\frac{2}{2}=\frac{3}{3}=\frac{4}{4}=\frac{5}{5}=\frac{6}{6}=\frac{9}{9}=\frac{10}{10}=1$

3. Encourage the placing of the fractions on a fraction number line (in fraction form or decimal form or both).

Decimals and fractions 1 ⑱

● ● ● ● ● ●

To change a fraction to a decimal **divide** $\div$
the top number (called the numerator)
by the bottom number (called the denominator).

Examples $\frac{1}{4}$ ⟹ press 1 ÷ 4 =

	0.25

$\frac{5}{8}$ ⟹ press 5 ÷ 8 =

	0.625

Change each fraction to a decimal.
Record the displays **in your own writing**.

$\frac{1}{2}$ =

$\frac{3}{8}$ =

$\frac{1}{4}$ =

$\frac{4}{4}$ =

$\frac{1}{8}$ =

$\frac{4}{8}$ =

$\frac{2}{2}$ =

$\frac{5}{8}$ =

$\frac{2}{4}$ =

$\frac{6}{8}$ =

$\frac{2}{8}$ =

$\frac{7}{8}$ =

$\frac{3}{4}$ =

$\frac{8}{8}$ =

Ring in different colours the sets of fractions that make
the **same** decimal.

....

Name _____ Class _____

CACULATOR CONVERSION OF FRACTIONS TO DECIMALS.
OBSERVATION OF EQUIVALENT FRACTIONS.

© Unwin Hyman
Calculated to Please 3

Decimals and fractions 2 ⑲

●●●●●●

To change a fraction to a decimal **divide** ⊡
the top number (called the numerator)
by the bottom number (called the denominator).

Examples $\frac{3}{10}$ ⟹ press 3 ÷ 1 0 = | 0.3 |

   $\frac{2}{5}$ ⟹ press 2 ÷ 5 = | 0.4 |

Change each fraction to a decimal.
Record the displays **in your own writing**.

$\frac{1}{5}$ = [   ] $\frac{5}{5}$ = [   ]

$\frac{1}{10}$ = [   ] $\frac{5}{10}$ = [   ]

$\frac{2}{5}$ = [   ] $\frac{6}{10}$ = [   ]

$\frac{2}{10}$ = [   ] $\frac{7}{10}$ = [   ]

$\frac{3}{5}$ = [   ] $\frac{8}{10}$ = [   ]

$\frac{3}{10}$ = [   ] $\frac{9}{10}$ = [   ]

$\frac{4}{5}$ = [   ] $\frac{10}{10}$ = [   ]

$\frac{4}{10}$ = [   ] $\frac{8}{20}$ = [   ]

Ring in different colours the sets of fractions that make
the **same** decimal.

. . . .»

Name _____   Class _____

CALCULATOR CONVERSION OF FRACTIONS TO DECIMALS.
OBSERVATION OF EQUIVALENT FRACTIONS.

© Unwin Hyman
Calculated to Please 3

● ○ ● ● ● ●

To change a fraction to a decimal **divide** ÷
the top number (called the numerator)
by the bottom number (called the denominator).

Examples $\frac{1}{3}$ ⟹ press [1][÷][3][=] | 0.3333333 |

$\frac{2}{9}$ ⟹ press [2][÷][9][=] | 0.2222222 |

Change each fraction to a decimal.
Record the displays **in your own writing**.

$\frac{1}{3}$ =

$\frac{1}{6}$ =

$\frac{1}{9}$ =

$\frac{2}{3}$ =

$\frac{2}{6}$ =

$\frac{2}{9}$ =

$\frac{3}{3}$ =

$\frac{3}{6}$ =

$\frac{3}{9}$ =

$\frac{4}{6}$ =

$\frac{4}{9}$ =

$\frac{5}{6}$ =

$\frac{5}{9}$ =

$\frac{6}{6}$ =

$\frac{6}{9}$ =

$\frac{7}{9}$ =

$\frac{8}{9}$ =

$\frac{9}{9}$ =

Ring in different colours the sets of fractions that make
the **same** decimal.

. . . .

Name _____

Class _____

CALCULATOR CONVERSION OF FRACTIONS TO DECIMALS.
OBSERVATION OF EQUIVALENT FRACTIONS.

Making waves ㉑

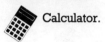

Activity/Purpose

The purposes of the activity are to develop the child's ability to
count on and count back in decimals, and to practise associated
estimation skills. The child estimates the likely 'last' number, given
a starter and the technique of adding (or subtracting) a given
constant a set number of times. The calculator is set to create the
sequence and the numbers are recorded.

Previous mathematical knowledge and skill required

Experience of decimal place value (one place of decimals only).
Familiarity with addition and subtraction of simple decimals.
Familiarity with the constant function of the calculator.

Notes on using the page

Ensure that the child estimates the final numbers **before** keying in
the sequence. With less able children it is advisable to 'talk
through' one example before allowing independent use of the
page.
Note that the keying in can omit the ⓪ from the key sequence.
However, it is advised that this be included in early stages of
calculator decimal work.
Briefly discuss the fact that the calculator display shows the
decimal point in a different place than in print or handwriting, 2. 1
rather than 2·1.

EQUIPMENT

Calculator.

Answers/Solutions

1.	0·7	0·8	0·9	1·0	1·1	1·2	1·3	1·4
2.	1·7	1·5	1·3	1·1	0·9	0·7	0·5	0·3
3.	1·2	1·5	1·8	2·1	2·4	2·7	3	3·3
4.	2·9	2·5	2·1	1·7	1·3	0·9	0·5	0·1
5.	0·8	1·3	1·8	2·3	2·8	3·3	3·8	4·3
6.	4·7	4·1	3·5	2·9	2·3	1·7	1·1	0·5
7.	3·1	3·8	4·5	5·2	5·9	6·6	7·3	8

ADDITIONAL ACTIVITIES
EXTENSIONS

1. Discuss the similarities with
counting on and back in the
whole numbers 1 to 9.

2. Discuss the child's judgement
about how many guesses were
good guesses. What constitutes a
good guess?

3. Encourage the child to reverse
each of the sequences, i.e.
subtract 0·1; add 0·2; and so on.
Encourage discussion of the
inverse nature of addition and
subtraction.

Ⓝ Ⓞ Ⓣ Ⓔ Ⓢ

Making waves

Make a 'good guess' at the **last** number before you start.

Set the calculator to:  **Fill in the numbers on the waves**

1. add 0·1

Press $\boxed{0}\boxed{\cdot}\boxed{1}\boxed{+}\boxed{+}\boxed{=}\boxed{0}$

then the first number, then $\boxed{=}$

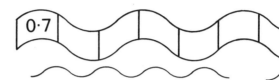

2. subtract 0·2

Press $\boxed{0}\boxed{\cdot}\boxed{2}\boxed{-}\boxed{-}\boxed{=}\boxed{0}$

then the first number, then $\boxed{=}$

3. add 0·3

Press $\boxed{0}\boxed{\cdot}\boxed{3}\boxed{+}\boxed{+}\boxed{=}\boxed{0}$

then the first number, then $\boxed{=}$

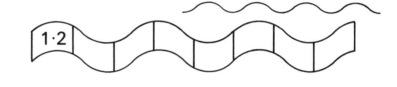

4. subtract 0·4

Press $\boxed{0}\boxed{\cdot}\boxed{4}\boxed{-}\boxed{-}\boxed{=}\boxed{0}$

then the first number, then $\boxed{=}$

5. add 0·5

Press $\boxed{0}\boxed{\cdot}\boxed{5}\boxed{+}\boxed{+}\boxed{=}\boxed{0}$

then the first number, then $\boxed{=}$

6. subtract 0·6

Press $\boxed{0}\boxed{\cdot}\boxed{6}\boxed{-}\boxed{-}\boxed{=}\boxed{0}$

then the first number, then $\boxed{=}$

7. add 0·7

Press $\boxed{0}\boxed{\cdot}\boxed{7}\boxed{+}\boxed{+}\boxed{=}\boxed{0}$

then the first number, then $\boxed{=}$

How many of your guesses were 'good guesses'? ☐

. . . .

Name _____ Class _____

USING A CALCULATOR CONSTANT TO COUNT ON AND BACK IN DECIMAL
AMOUNTS. DEVELOPING ESTIMATION SKILLS.

© Unwin Hyman
Calculated to Please 3

Deci-grids ㉒

● ● ● ● ● ●

Activity/Purpose

The purpose of the activity is to encourage the child to develop care in keying in decimals and to examine the patterns which emerge when a restricted number of operations is used.

The child begins with a given number and successively adds or subtracts given decimals to reach an 'answer'. Because of the structure, the last number is always directly related to the starting number.

EQUIPMENT

 Calculator.

Previous mathematical knowledge and skill required

Experience of addition and subtraction of decimals to one place.

Notes on using the page

Check first that the child is capable of reading the decimals and of keying in using the decimal-point key.

Allow the child to use one or both of these possible methods:

(a) *Horizontal*
$\boxed{2}\boxed{+}\boxed{0}\boxed{.}\boxed{2}\boxed{=}\boxed{-}\boxed{0}\boxed{.}\boxed{5}\ldots$
or $\boxed{2}\boxed{+}\boxed{.}\boxed{2}\boxed{=}\boxed{-}\boxed{.}\boxed{5}\ldots$
or $\boxed{2}\boxed{+}\boxed{.}\boxed{2}\boxed{-}\boxed{.}\boxed{5}\ldots$
or a combination of these, depending upon ability.

(b) *Vertical*, i.e. set up the constant for **add 0·2**.
$\boxed{0}\boxed{.}\boxed{2}\boxed{+}\boxed{+}\boxed{=}\boxed{0}$ (starting number) $\boxed{=}$
Fill in the first column, then set up the next constant and repeat.

Require the child to note and record the basic pattern by completing the sentence on the page.

● ● ● ● ● ●

Answers/Solutions

2	2·2	1·7	3	2·4	4·5	4
3	3·2	2·7	4	3·4	5·5	5
5	5·2	4·7	6	5·4	7·5	7
7	7·2	6·7	8	7·4	9·5	9

10	10·2	9·7	11	10·4	12·5	12
12	12·2	11·7	13	12·4	14·5	14
15	15·2	14·7	16	15·4	17·5	17
18	18·2	17·7	19	18·4	20·5	20
21	21·2	20·7	22	21·4	23·5	23

ADDITIONAL ACTIVITIES
EXTENSIONS

1. Discuss the use of the alternative methods shown in the notes opposite.

2. Discuss the vertical patterns which emerge, i.e. always the same decimal 'part' of the answer.

3. Make an unnumbered blank of this activity and use it to encourage the child to examine other starters (including decimals), and other chains of operations.

○ Ⓝ ⓞ Ⓣ Ⓔ Ⓢ

Deci-grids

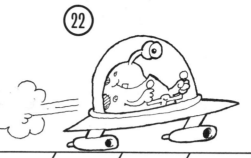

Use your calculator to help you.
Fill in the missing numbers

Start with these numbers.	First +0·2	then −0·5	then +1·3	then −0·6	then +2·1	then −0·5
2 ▶	2·2	1·7	3	2·4	4·5	4
3 ▶						
5 ▶						
7 ▶						
10 ▶						
12 ▶						
15 ▶						
18 ▶						
21 ▶						

Finish this sentence.
The last number is always ☐ larger than the 'start' number.

....

Name _____   Class _____

PATTERNS INVOLVING DECIMALS.

Bingo (add, take and times)

Activity/Purpose

The purpose of the games is to encourage estimation skills (including 'rounding') in simple decimals and to develop speed and efficiency in keying in decimal calculations.

The games are based on **Bingo** and **Cover-up**, in which a restricted choice of starting numbers produce an 'answer' on the bingo sheet. The object of each game is to be the first to achieve a line of five counters, horizontally, vertically or diagonally.

Previous mathematical knowledge and skill required

Experience of addition, subtraction, and multiplication of one-place decimals.
Familiarity with the idea of rounding and estimation as a prelude to calculation.

Notes on using the pages

Please note that not all the pages can be used at the same ability level. Less able children find difficulty with estimation of products of two decimals, particularly when one of the decimals is less than 1.

Check that the children understand the rules and the restricted choice of numbers to use (in the choosing list). The use of a single calculator, which is shared, is to encourage checking of calculator inputs and outputs by both players.

EQUIPMENT

 1 Calculator.

 A copy of the pupil page for each player.

 Some *small* counters.

ADDITIONAL ACTIVITIES EXTENSIONS

1. Discuss the link between estimation and rounding, in decimals and in whole numbers.

2. Investigate with the child how many different computations (but not necessarily answers) can be made from each given set of 8 numbers (answer 7+6+5+4+3+2+1=28).

Links with our own maths scheme

Other activities and extensions used

General evaluation of the children's work

Bingo - add

Play with a friend.
You need: a bingo sheet each
and some counters.
You must: share a calculator.

Rules
Take turns to:
1. Pick 2 numbers from the choosing list.
2. **Add** them.
3. Put a counter on the answer if it is on the bingo sheet.

The first to get a **straight** line of 5 counters in any direction is the winner!

Choosing list:	1·7	2·2	2·8	3·1
	3·5	1·9	2·7	2·4

5·8	4·5	5·5	4·6	3·9
5·3	4·1	5·7	5·9	4·4
4·8	6·3	4·7	5·2	5·1
4·6	5·0	5·4	3·6	4·9
6·6	4·3	3·6	4·1	6·2

Name _____

Class _____

BINGO GAME FOR 2 PLAYERS: ADDITION OF ONE PLACE OF DECIMALS.

Play with a friend.
You need: a bingo sheet each
and some counters.
You must: share a calculator.

The first to get a **straight** line of 5 counters
in any direction is the winner!

Rules
Take turns to:
1. Pick 2 numbers from the choosing list.
2. **Subtract** the smaller from the larger.
3. Put a counter on the answer if it is on the bingo sheet.

Choosing list:		0·3	5·5	0·8
3·8	2·7	4·2	3·3	1·9

1·3	3·4	1·9	0·9	2·4
4·7	2·5	2·8	3·5	1·5
0·5	1·7	3·9	1·6	0·6
2·3	1·1	3·0	0·8	3·6
1·4	5·2	0·4	2·2	1·9

Name _____   Class _____

BINGO GAME FOR 2 PLAYERS: SUBTRACTION OF ONE PLACE OF DECIMALS.

Bingo-times

Play with a friend.
You need: a bingo sheet each
and some counters.
You must: share a calculator.

The first to get a **straight** line of 5 counters
in any direction is the winner!

Rules
Take turns to:
1. Pick 2 numbers from the choosing list.
2. **Multiply** them.
3. Put a counter on the answer if it is on the bingo sheet.

Choosing list:		2·3	2·1	0·7
1·5	0·9	0·3	1·8	1·4

0·21	0·69	1·89	2·7	1·47
1·35	2·94	0·63	2·07	0·5
2·52	0·27	0·98	1·26	3·15
0·54	3·78	1·61	1·05	4·14
3·45	1·62	3·22	0·42	2·1

. . . .

Name _____ Class _____

BINGO GAME FOR 2 PLAYERS: MULTIPLICATION OF ONE PLACE DECIMALS.

Boxers! ㉖

● ● ● ● ● ●

Activity/Purpose

This is a puzzle requiring the matching of a fraction and its decimal equivalent, given the digits but not their location. The child uses the calculator to test alternative ratios (fractions) to find which produce a true number sentence.

Previous mathematical knowledge and skill required

Use of a calculator to find decimal equivalents of given fractions. Experience of decimal place value.

Notes on using the page

It is essential that work on this page is preceded by experience of creating decimals from fractions.

Ensure that the child understands the technique for finding the solution, that is, a combination of rounding/estimation, previous knowledge, and a trial-and-error approach. The examples can be taken and examined in any order.

EQUIPMENT

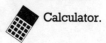 Calculator.

● ● ● ● ● ●

Answers/Solutions

1. $\frac{4}{8}=0\cdot50$
2. $\frac{8}{5}=1\cdot6$
3. $\frac{9}{8}=1\cdot125$
4. $\frac{7}{10}=0\cdot7$
5. $\frac{7}{4}=1\cdot75$
6. $\frac{9}{6}=1\cdot5$
7. $\frac{9}{2}=4\cdot5$
8. $\frac{7}{2}=3\cdot5$
9. $\frac{6}{5}=1\cdot2$
10. $\frac{6}{8}=0\cdot75$

ADDITIONAL ACTIVITIES
EXTENSIONS

1. Encourage the child to find one or more fraction equivalents for a given two-digit decimal.

2. Encourage the child to change the fraction numbers, but so that they still match the same decimal.

Ⓝ Ⓞ Ⓣ Ⓔ Ⓢ

Links with our own maths scheme

Other activities and extensions used

General evaluation of the children's work

Boxers!

26

Use only the digits you are given.
Put them in the squares to make a fraction **and** a decimal
that are **equivalent**. ('Equivalent' means they have the same value.)

1. Use only (0, 4, 5, 8.

$\dfrac{4}{8} = \boxed{0} \cdot \boxed{5}$

2. Use only (1, 5, 6, 8

$\dfrac{\square}{\square} = \square \cdot \square$

3. Use only (1, 2, 5, 8, 9

$\dfrac{\square}{\square} = \square \cdot \boxed{1}\,\square\,\square$

4. Use only (0, 0, 1, 7, 7

$\dfrac{\square}{\square\square} = \square \cdot \square$

5. Use only (1, 4, 5, 7

$\dfrac{\square}{\square} = \square \cdot \boxed{7}\,\square$

6. Use only (1, 5, 6, 9

$\dfrac{\square}{\square} = \square \cdot \square$

7. Use only (2, 4, 5, 9

$\dfrac{\square}{\square} = \square \cdot \square$

8. Use only (2, 3, 5, 7

$\dfrac{\square}{\square} = \square \cdot \square$

9. Use only (1, 2, 5, 6

$\dfrac{\square}{\square} = \square \cdot \square$

10. Use only (0, 5, 6, 7, 8

$\dfrac{\square}{\square} = \square \cdot \square\square$

Name _____   Class _____

PUZZLE: MATCHING FRACTIONS AND DECIMAL EQUIVALENTS.

Changing places ㉗

● ● ● ● ● ●

Activity/Purpose

The purpose of the activity is to use the constant function to show how the place value of the digits changes in an observable sequence when a number is divided by 10. The children discuss this.

The child sets the constant, keys in the given number, reduces it by a factor of 10 by using the [=] and records the displays in the order in which they appear.

Previous mathematical knowledge and skill required

Experience of decimal place value 'labelling'.
Experience of 'reading' large numbers.
Familiarity with the constant function of the calculator.

Notes on using the page

Ensure that the child is familiar with the constant function, or is able to key in the division manually.
Discuss the 'reading' of the given number and the titles of the unlabelled columns.
Encourage the child to guess the next line before it is created in the display and recorded.

EQUIPMENT

 Calculator.

 Centimetre squared paper.

ADDITIONAL ACTIVITIES EXTENSIONS

1. Discuss the visual and numerical pattern which emerges.

2. Discuss what happens to the numbers which 'fall off' the right-hand end of the sequence.

3. Encourage the child to 'reverse' part of the sequence by multiplying by a constant of 10 from, say, 0·123 456 7.

4. Encourage the child to investigate the pattern which emerges if he or she divides 12 345 678 by 100, or by 1000.

5. Encourage investigation of multiplying 0·123 456 7 by 100 or 1000.

6. Encourage investigation of other numbers, such as 5, multiplying and/or dividing to change the direction of place values.

 N O T E S

Links with our own maths scheme

Other activities and extensions used

General evaluation of the children's work

Changing places

27

Set your calculator to divide by 10
like this: ①⓪÷÷=⓪

Key in 12 345 678.

Press = again and again.

After each press, record the display on the chart.

	Millions			Th	H	T	U •	$\frac{1}{10}$	$\frac{1}{100}$	$\frac{1}{1000}$				
1	2	3	4	5	6	7	8 •							
							•							
							•							
							•							
							•							
							•							
							•							
							•							
							•							
							•							
							•							
							•							
							•							
							•							
							•							
							•							

Name _____   Class _____

USE OF A CALCULATOR TO CREATE THE SEQUENCE OF PLACE-VALUE
CHANGES WHEN DIVIDING REPEATEDLY BY 10.

© Unwin Hyman
Calculated to Please 3

1089 or not?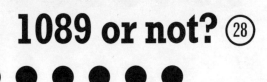

Activity/Purpose

The purpose of the activity is to encourage calculator use for fast consideration of a range of examples in a number investigation. A hypothesis about the possible 'rules' is then made by the child, using the examples he or she has chosen and worked. The hypothesis can be tested for a wide range of numbers.

Previous mathematical knowledge and skill required

Understanding of the term 'digit'.
Experience of addition and subtraction of 3-digit numbers.

Notes on using the page

Encourage the child to work the first example and have it checked to ensure understanding of the sequence of instructions. Then encourage the child to try different starting numbers in order to see which result in which 'answers' after the given sequence. It may be useful to give each child two copies of the page to allow all possibilities to be tested. Ask the child to **record** the numbers which emerge and to attempt an 'own-words' description of his or her findings, on the back of the page.

Answers/Solutions

1089 is reached if the difference between the first and last digits of the starting number is 2 or more.

198 is reached if the difference between the first and last digits is 1.

0 is reached if the number is a palindrome, e.g. 232 or 333.

EQUIPMENT

Calculator.

ADDITIONAL ACTIVITIES EXTENSIONS

The 'subtract the smaller number from the larger number' instruction is easily handled using a calculator for re-entering the digits in the required order. However it is not necessary if the calculator has a $\boxed{+/-}$ key, which is used as follows: Child chooses, say, 123, and reverses the digits (321). The first number can be kept in the calculator and this sequence is used:
123 $\boxed{+/-}$ $\boxed{+}$ 321 $\boxed{=}$

Ⓝ Ⓞ Ⓣ Ⓔ Ⓢ

Links with our own maths scheme

Other activities and extensions used

General evaluation of the children's work

1089 or not?

28

Write a three-digit number.
Reverse the order of the digits.

Subtract the smaller number
from the larger number.

Reverse the order of the digits.

Add the last two numbers.

Use your calculator to help you work faster!

There are only **three** possible answers: 1089 or 198 or 0.

Try different starting numbers.
What special things about them give the different answers?

Write about your discovery on the back of this page.

Name _____ Class _____

NUMBER INVESTIGATION USING A CALCULATOR FOR SPEED.

© Unwin Hyman
Calculated to Please 3

Come to the point ㉙

Activity/Purpose

The purpose of the activity is to develop the child's awareness of the inverse/reciprocal relationship of multiplication and division in a decimal context.

Given the 'common' decimals 0·5, 0·25, 1·5 and 0·75, the child needs to find pairs of whole numbers which, when divided, produce the given decimal.

EQUIPMENT

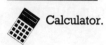 Calculator.

Previous mathematical knowledge and skill required

Experience of multiplication and division of whole numbers. Awareness of the concept of a decimal as equivalent to a fraction or ratio.

Notes on using the page

It is likely that the inexperienced child will use a trial-and-error method of finding the missing numbers. This is a perfectly sound strategy but time consuming. It would therefore be worth discussing the method of calculating the missing numbers if the child becomes frustrated, i.e.: given the **first** number, the second is found by **dividing** the first by, say 0·5; given the **second** number, the first is found by **multiplying** the second by, say 0·5.

Answers/Solutions

All make 0·5	All make 0·25
1 ÷ 2	1 ÷ 4
2 ÷ 4	3 ÷ 12
3 ÷ 6	2 ÷ 8
4 ÷ 8	5 ÷ 20
16 ÷ 32	16 ÷ 64
100 ÷ 200	25 ÷ 100
33 ÷ 66	96 ÷ 384
225 ÷ 450	100 ÷ 400
634 ÷ 1268	140 ÷ 560

All make 1·5	All make 0·75
3 ÷ 2	3 ÷ 4
9 ÷ 6	9 ÷ 12
30 ÷ 20	36 ÷ 48
24 ÷ 16	24 ÷ 32
75 ÷ 50	54 ÷ 72
15 ÷ 10	72 ÷ 96
225 ÷ 150	75 ÷ 100
150 ÷ 100	750 ÷ 1000
999 ÷ 666	600 ÷ 800

ADDITIONAL ACTIVITIES EXTENSIONS

1. Encourage the child to build sequences which will produce the given decimals, e.g. 1÷2 → 2÷4 → 3÷6 → 4÷8 → 5÷10

2. If not already discussed, consider with the child the method described opposite, under Notes.

3. Examine situations where the zero is automatically placed into the display or is eliminated from the display, e.g. key in ·5 and the display shows 0.5; key in 0·50 and press = and the last zero is eliminated.

Come to the point

29

Fill in the missing numbers.

Use your calculator.

all make 0·5

all make 0·5

1	÷		=
	÷	4	=
3	÷		=
	÷	8	=
16	÷		=
100	÷		=
	÷	66	=
225	÷		=
	÷	1268	=

all make 0·25

all make 0·25

	÷	4	=
3	÷		=
	÷	8	=
5	÷		=
16	÷		=
	÷	100	=
96	÷		=
100	÷		=
	÷	560	=

all make 1·5

all make 1·5

3	÷		=
9	÷		=
30	÷		=
	÷	16	=
	÷	50	=
15	÷		=
	÷	150	=
	÷	100	=
999	÷		=

all make 0·75

all make 0·75

3	÷		=
9	÷		=
36	÷		=
	÷	32	=
	÷	72	=
72	÷		=
	÷	100	=
750	÷		=
600	÷		=

Name _____ Class _____

USING A CALCULATOR TO DISCOVER RATIOS (FRACTIONS) WHICH PRODUCE COMMON DECIMALS.

© Unwin Hyman
Calculated to Please 3

Figure skating ㉚

Activity/Purpose

The purpose of the activity is to use a 'television sport' topic to encourage the use of a calculator in ordering, adding and dividing decimals. The child follows the instructions and calculates the final mark for each competitor; and then orders the decimals to find first, second and third places.

Previous mathematical knowledge and skill required

Experience of decimal place value.
Experience of the concept of an average as a **mean** of a set of numbers.

Notes on using the page

Briefly discuss the approach to scoring used in multi-judge competitions.
Ensure that the child has an understanding of the reason why the total marks are divided by 14.
Note that the final score produces a full display of figures to 7 decimal places. However, only the first two places of decimals need to be considered.

Answers/Solutions

Annie Seed	Technical ability	Total	65·2
(Bronze medal)	Artistic merit	Total	60·2
	Average mark	8·95	
Jo King	Technical ability	Total	59·7
(Silver medal)	Artistic merit	Total	65·8
	Average mark	8·96	
Sue Purr	Technical ability	Total	63·3
(Gold medal)	Artistic merit	Total	63·2
	Average mark	9·03	

ADDITIONAL ACTIVITIES EXTENSIONS

1. Discuss the reasons why the highest and lowest scores are deleted (to reduce bias).

2. Discuss reasons why two aspects of performance are marked separately.

3. Encourage the child to see that the problem could be done using whole number equivalents (e.g. 9·3 treated as 93) without relative effect on the final average. Marks out of 10 are merely one-tenth of the size of marks out of 100.

4. Encourage the child to check scores given in televised skating competitions. (Diving competitions are marked in a similar way.)

5. Discuss whether rounding the scores to the nearest whole number would allow a reasonably accurate **estimate** of the relative scores to be made.

Figure skating

30

In skating competitions **nine** judges give marks.
They each give a mark out of 10 for technical ability,
and a mark out of 10 for artistic merit.

For each skater the referee then:

1. crosses out the highest and lowest marks in **each** section;
2. adds together the marks that are left;
3. divides the answer by 14 to find the **average** mark.
4. The skater with the highest average mark wins!

Who got the medals in this competition?

Annie Seed		Jo King		Sue Purr	
Technical ability	Artistic merit	Technical ability	Artistic merit	Technical ability	Artistic merit
9·3	8·6	8·3	9·5	8·9	9·1
9·6	8·7	8·9	9·7	9·2	8·7
9·1	8·6	9·0	9·1	9·0	9·0
9·0	8·5	8·3	8·9	9·6	9·3
9·3	8·9	8·4	9·6	8·2	9·3
9·5	8·7	8·6	9·7	9·1	8·2
9·7	8·8	8·2	9·3	8·7	8·9
9·2	8·2	8·7	9·4	9·2	9·1
9·2	8·3	8·5	9·2	9·2	9·1

Name _____   Class _____

USE OF A CALCULATOR TO ORDER, ADD AND DIVIDE DECIMALS.

© Unwin Hyman
Calculated to Please 3

Party Planner ㉛

Activity/Purpose

The purpose of the activity is to use the calculator as an aid to real problem solving, involving money. The activity is for two children, working together so that discussion can (and should) take place.

The children decide about, and record, costs for a party. Then they use a calculator to find out costs for a given number of people; and the number who could attend if the budget was limited.

EQUIPMENT

Calculator.

Previous mathematical knowledge and skill required

Experience of the four rules of number applied to money. Familiarity with the constant functions of the calculator.

Notes on using the page

Part A is the basic data, created by the children. Ensure that they understand that the first two columns are costs **per person**.
The first column might include items such as:

crisps   20p
cola   30p
sandwiches   40p

Estimated costs should be used.

The **third** column is a set of **fixed** costs and might include video hire or some new records or tapes or CDs.

Part B
The **total** costs is made up of fixed costs and variable costs.
So the total cost for 1 person might be

$$(2{\cdot}50)+1{\cdot}50+50p=£4{\cdot}50$$
for 2 persons
$$(2{\cdot}50)+3{\cdot}00+£1 \;=£6{\cdot}50$$
and so on.

The variable costs could be created by use of the constant function of the calculator: (total variable cost) $\boxed{+}\ \boxed{+}\ \boxed{=}\ \boxed{=}\ \ldots$

Part C
The data here can be created from the data in part **B**. It is important to see that only **whole numbers** of people can attend! A certain amount of 'change' can thus be expected.

ADDITIONAL ACTIVITIES EXTENSIONS

1. Plan a picnic in the same way, noting that the cost of a 'whole' coach is a fixed cost.

2. Draw graphs of the values shown in parts **B** and **C**.

 (N) (O) (T) (E) (S)

Party planner

Work with a friend.
Plan the cost of a party.
Use a calculator when you can.

A

Costs					
Food and drink for each person		'Take home' presents for each person		Entertainment (e.g. video hire)	
What?	Cost per person	What?	Cost per person	What?	Cost
Total for each person		Total for each person		Total cost of entertainment	

This total is **fixed**.
It stays the same no matter how many people come.

B How much would a party cost for these numbers of people?

Number of people	1	2	3	4	5	6	7	8	9	10
Total cost										

C How many people could be at the party for each of these total amounts spent?

Number of people										
Amount spent	£5	£10	£15	£20	£25	£30	£35	£40	£45	£50

. . . .

Name _____   Class _____

CALCULATOR-AIDED PROBLEM SOLVING.

© Unwin Hyman
Calculated to Please 3

Memory

Activity/Purpose

Probably the most neglected keys on a basic calculator are the
memory keys, which allow part of a calculation to be stored and
retrieved. The purpose of the activity is to illustrate and
investigate the use of the memory in two or more part
computations. The use of the memory (once it can be trusted!) is a
valuable aid to calculator-supported problem solving.

Previous mathematical knowledge and skill required

Experience of brackets in multi-part computations.
Experience of estimation/rounding.

Notes on using the page

The key sequence, although extremely rewarding in terms of
calculator use, can be a little confusing at first. Therefore
discussion and checking of the worked example is advisable.
Please note that the third step, pressing $\boxed{\text{CE}}$ to clear the rest of the
calculator, can be omitted without detriment. It is advised that it
be included to separate overtly the various parts of the calculation.
Encourage the child to be careful about the signs (operations)
used in the examples.

Answers/Solutions

$(57+23)-(92-19)$
$57\boxed{+}23\boxed{=}\boxed{\text{M+}}\boxed{\text{CE}}92\boxed{-}19\boxed{=}\boxed{\text{M-}}\boxed{\text{MR}}\boxed{\text{MC}} \rightarrow$ **7**

$(13\times24)+(6\times14)$
$13\boxed{\times}24\boxed{=}\boxed{\text{M+}}\boxed{\text{CE}}6\boxed{\times}14\boxed{=}\boxed{\text{M+}}\boxed{\text{MR}}\boxed{\text{MC}} \rightarrow$ **396**

$99-(153\div17)$
$99\boxed{\text{M+}}\boxed{\text{CE}}153\boxed{\div}17\boxed{=}\boxed{\text{M-}}\boxed{\text{MR}}\boxed{\text{MC}} \rightarrow$ **90**

EQUIPMENT

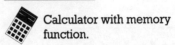 Calculator with memory
function.

ADDITIONAL ACTIVITIES EXTENSIONS

1. Encourage wider use of the
   memory in general multi-step
   calculations, e.g.:
   $\frac{3}{4}+\frac{4}{9} \rightarrow (3\div4)+(4\div9)$.
2. Compare speed of computation
   using memory and non-memory
   methods.

Ⓝ Ⓞ Ⓣ Ⓔ Ⓢ

Links with our own maths scheme

Other activities and extensions used

General evaluation of the children's work

Memory

Sometimes you need to solve part of a calculation, to use later.
Your calculator can do it for you.

You need these keys
on your calculator.
| M+ | M− | MR | MC |

21 − (7 + 3)

Memory code

2	1		puts 21 in display
M+			puts 21 in memory
CE			clears rest of calculator
7	+	3	=	works out the part in brackets
M−			subtracts bracket answer from number in memory
MR			tells you what is now in memory
MC			clears memory

These may be on the **same** key.

11.

Make up **memory codes** for these calculations.

(57 + 23) − (92 − 19)	(13 × 24) + (6 × 14)	99 − (153 ÷ 17)

Name _____

Class _____

USING THE CALCULATOR MEMORY.

Ferry good money! ㉝

Activity/Purpose

The purpose of the activity is to develop the child's facility with the calculator memory in a 'money' context. The child uses the calculator-memory method (see the previous spread *Memory*) to total takings on a ferry. The data are then ranked in order of takings and a graph is drawn of the results.

Previous mathematical knowledge and skill required

Experience of the calculator memory.
Familiarity with the drawing of bar-charts.
Ability to order numbers in hundreds, tens and units.

Notes on using the page

Ensure familiarity with the calculator memory to ease the burden of computation, e.g. Morning crossing:
$495 \boxed{\times} 2 \boxed{=} \boxed{M+} 71 \boxed{\times} 10 \boxed{=} \boxed{M+} \ldots$

Encourage **estimation** of the takings for each category before using the calculator.

Answers/Solutions

	Morning crossing	Evening crossing	Totals
People	£990	£1244	2234
Cars	710	680	1390
Coaches	405	315	720
Caravans	154	165	319
Motorbikes	196	112	308
Pedal bikes	162	147	309
Totals	£2617	£2663	

Ranking

1st People	2nd Cars	3rd Coaches
4th Caravans	5th Pedal bikes	6th Motorbikes

ADDITIONAL ACTIVITIES EXTENSIONS

1. Discuss the scale of fares. Given the relative sizes of the vehicles, is the charge for a coach too high, or too low?

2. Encourage inference from the data and the graph that is drawn. Is it a summer day? Is it a small island?

Ⓝ Ⓞ Ⓣ Ⓔ Ⓢ

Links with our own maths scheme

Other activities and extensions used

General evaluation of the children's work

Ferry good money!

The ferry *Loadsamoney* takes holiday makers to the perfect island of Orinoco. It has everything! But it costs a lot to get there.

Fares: *one way only*	
People on foot	£2
Cars	£10
Coaches	£45
Caravans	£11
Motobikes	£7
Pedal bikes	£3

Loadsamoney does one crossing in the morning and returns in the evening.

1. Finish off the Captain's accounts for the day.

MORNING CROSSING		
Item	Number	Takings £
People on foot	495	£
Cars	71	£
Coaches	9	£
Caravans	14	£
Motorbikes	28	£
Pedal bikes	54	£
Total takings		£

EVENING CROSSING		
Item	Number	Takings £
People on foot	622	£
Cars	68	£
Coaches	7	£
Caravans	15	£
Motorbikes	16	£
Pedal bikes	49	£
Total takings		£

Use the calculator memory to help here!

2. List the items in order of takings for the whole day.

1st	
2nd	
3rd	
4th	
5th	
6th	

3. On squared paper, draw a bar graph of your results.

4. Write 3 interesting things about your graph.

Name _____ Class _____

PROBLEM SOLVING USING A CALCULATOR (MEMORY).

© Unwin Hyman
Calculated to Please 3

Hop-scotch ㉞

● ● ● ● ● ●

Activity/Purpose

The purpose of the game (for 2 players) is to develop skills of
rounding, estimation, addition and subtraction of decimals.

Previous mathematical knowledge and skill required

Experience of rounding decimals.
Experience of addition and subtraction of decimals.

Notes on using the page

Check understanding of the rules before play commences. Note
that not all possible additions and subtractions are shown on the
hop-scotch grid. Point out that a 'go' will be wasted if random
guessing is attempted.
Point out, too, that remembering the opponent's correct
combinations will aid success in the homeward run of the game.

EQUIPMENT

 1 calculator (to encourage
mutual checking).

 Two small counters of
different colours.

ADDITIONAL ACTIVITIES
EXTENSIONS

Discuss the problem of rounding two
places of decimals – do we always
round to whole numbers, or to one
place of decimals. The similarity
with rounding whole numbers in
hundreds, tens and units can be
considered in the same way.

Make an unnumbered blank of the
page to use with whole numbers or
other decimal combinations,
depending on the ability of the
children.

Links with our own maths scheme

Other activities and extensions used

General evaluation of the children's work

Hop-scotch

Rules

1. Each pick an end to start.
2. Each put a counter on your start.
3. Take turns to:
   - pick two numbers from the 'choosers';
   - add **or** subtract them;
   - move to the next space – but **only if** it shows the answer you got.
4. The **winner** is the player who is the first to get to his or her opponent's start.

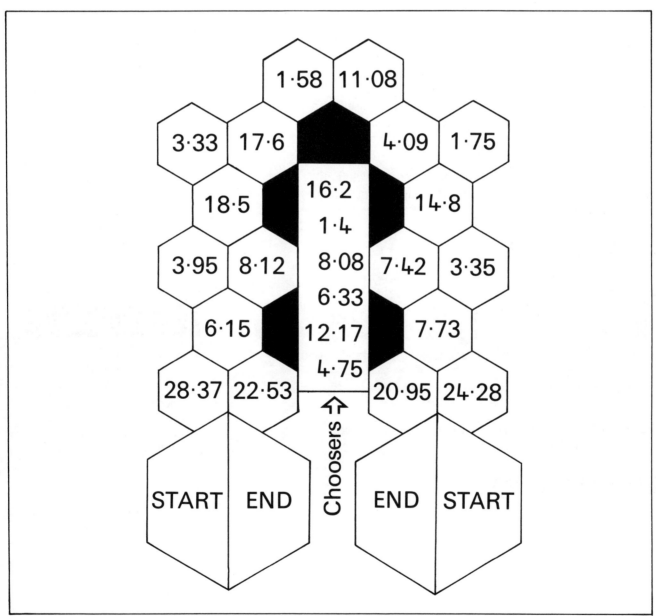

Name _____   Class _____

GAME INVOLVING ESTIMATION, ROUNDING, ADDITION AND SUBTRACTION OF DECIMALS.

© Unwin Hyman
Calculated to Please 3

Larger or smaller ㉟

Activity/Purpose

The purpose of the activity is to investigate the features of a series of decimals which, when multiplied together, produce either an increasing or decreasing series of 'answers'.

EQUIPMENT

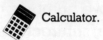 Calculator.

Previous mathematical knowledge and skill required

Ability to enter and multiply decimals on a calculator.
Experience of decimal 'place valuation'.

Notes on using the page

It would be advisable to work through the first example with the child to show how, indeed, the 'answers' after each full circuit become smaller. Then allow the child to investigate the other examples, using the calculator to reduce the burden of computation and speed up the development of a generalised 'rule'. After testing each shape and its set of numbers, the child should be able to form a conclusion as to why some increase and others decrease (see below for 'answer').

The latter half of the page requires a more specific solution: finding a combination of whole numbers and decimals which produce an answer of 1 when multiplied together in series.

Answers/Solutions

1. Smaller	**2.** Larger	**3.** Larger	**4.** Larger
5. Smaller	**6.** Larger	**7.** Smaller	**8.** Smaller

Answers get **larger** if the product of the four numbers after one circuit is **greater** than 1.
Answers get **smaller** if the product of the four numbers after one circuit is **less** than 1.

To achieve 1, a combination of numbers is required which 'cancel each other', e.g. 20×0·5×0·5×0·2.

ADDITIONAL ACTIVITIES EXTENSIONS

1. Encourage the child to create three examples which increase and three more which decrease.

2. Encourage the child to find four numbers or decimals which produce answers on the first circuit of 2, 3, 4, and so on.

Larger or smaller

35

Multiply each set of numbers, following the direction of the arrows.
At the end of each full circuit, write down the display number.
If the display numbers **at the end of each circuit** get **smaller** and **smaller**,
label the shape **S**.
If the display numbers **at the end of each circuit** get **larger** and **larger**,
label the shape **L**.

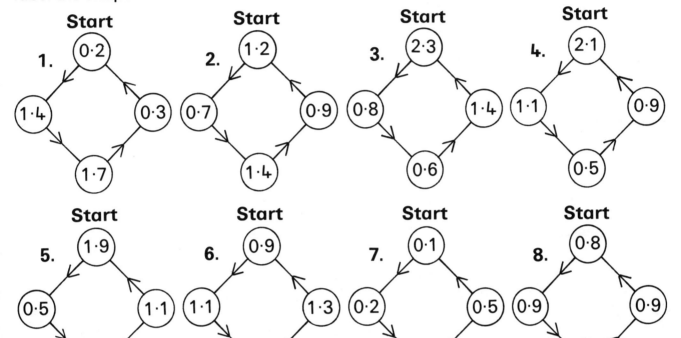

Answers get larger if_____

_____

Answers get smaller if_____

_____

On this shape, put numbers
that give the answer **1**
after one journey from
start back to start.

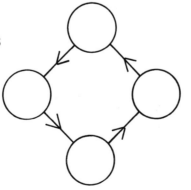

Name _____   Class _____

PUZZLE/INVESTIGATION OF MULTIPLICATION OF DECIMALS.

© Unwin Hyman
Calculated to Please 3

Twister (+), (−), (×) and (÷) ㊱–㊵

● ● ● ● ● ●

Activity/Purpose

The purpose of the activities on these pages is to reinforce the child's understanding of and ability in handling decimal place value. The first pages require the child to find a number which, when combined with the previous number, produces the following number. Each requires basic knowledge of the value of the digits in order to 'place' the decimal point or the new digit.

Previous mathematical knowledge and skill required

Experience of place-value recognition and 'naming'.
Ability to enter and add, subtract, multiply and divide decimals on a calculator.

Notes on using the pages

It is advisable to use the pages in the order in which they are presented, this being the sequence of conceptual difficulty. Assuming the previous knowledge specified, the instructions are self-explanatory.

● ● ● ● ● ●

Answers/Solutions

(+) 444·444 $\boxed{+10}$ 454·444 $\boxed{+0·02}$ 454·464
$\boxed{+100}$ 554·464 $\boxed{+0·5}$ 554·964 $\boxed{+0·006}$
554·970 $\boxed{+6}$ 560·970 $\boxed{+0·03}$ 561

(−) 765·432 $\boxed{-5}$ 760·432 $\boxed{-0·04}$ 760·392
$\boxed{-70}$ 690·392 $\boxed{-0·009}$ 690·383 $\boxed{-0·9}$
689·483 $\boxed{-400}$ 289·483 $\boxed{-6}$ 283·483

(×) 0·0003 $\boxed{\times 100}$ 0·03 $\boxed{\times 10}$ 0·3 $\boxed{\times 5}$ 1·5
$\boxed{\times 5}$ 7·5 $\boxed{\times 100}$ 750 $\boxed{\times 3}$ 2250 $\boxed{\times 4}$ 9000

(÷) 32000 $\boxed{\div 100}$ 320 $\boxed{\div 80}$ 4 $\boxed{\div 10}$ 0·4
$\boxed{\div 2}$ 0·2 $\boxed{\div 100}$ 0·002 $\boxed{\div 4}$ 0·0005
$\boxed{\div 5}$ 0·0001

The final sheet will receive a variety of responses. The answer should be proved to you by the child talking through what was done.

EQUIPMENT

 Calculator.

ADDITIONAL ACTIVITIES EXTENSIONS

1. Encourage the child to discuss/ talk through the sequence as soon as it has been done. In this way the inverse nature of addition and subtraction, and multiplication and division can be highlighted.

2. Encourage the child to reverse the sequence and check what is required to move from the head to the tail.

3. The final page of the set can be used to examine other starting numbers and ending numbers, by erasure of the given numbers and alteration of the given operation signs.

Twister (+)

Find and write the numbers **added** to make the twister right.

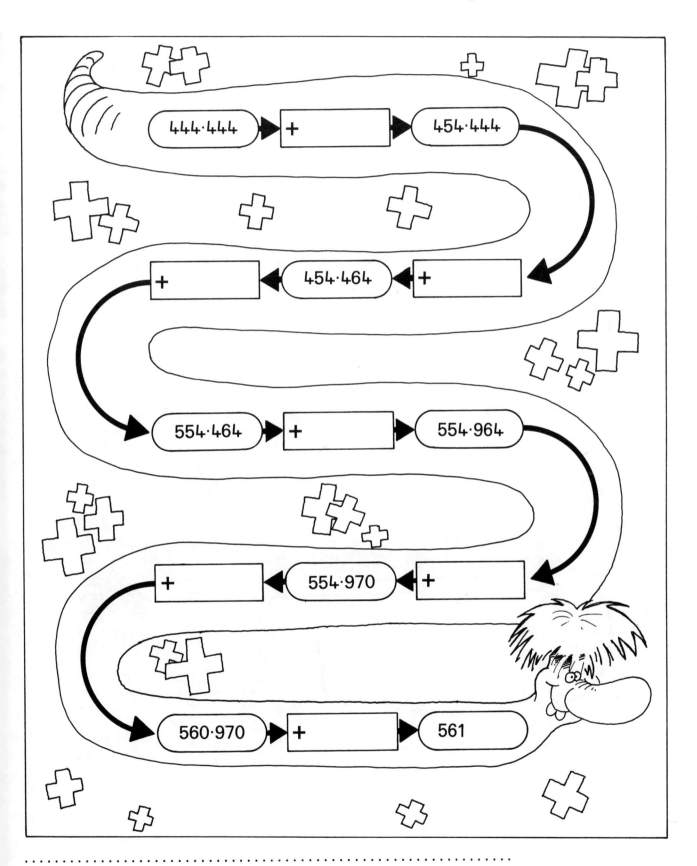

444·444 ▶ + ▶ 454·444

+ ◀ 454·464 ◀ +

554·464 ▶ + ▶ 554·964

+ ◀ 554·970 ◀ +

560·970 ▶ + ▶ 561

....

Name _____

Class _____

DECIMAL PLACE VALUE: PRACTICE ACTIVITY (ADDITION).

© Unwin Hyman
Calculated to Please 3

Twister (−)

Find and write the numbers **subtracted** to make the twister right.

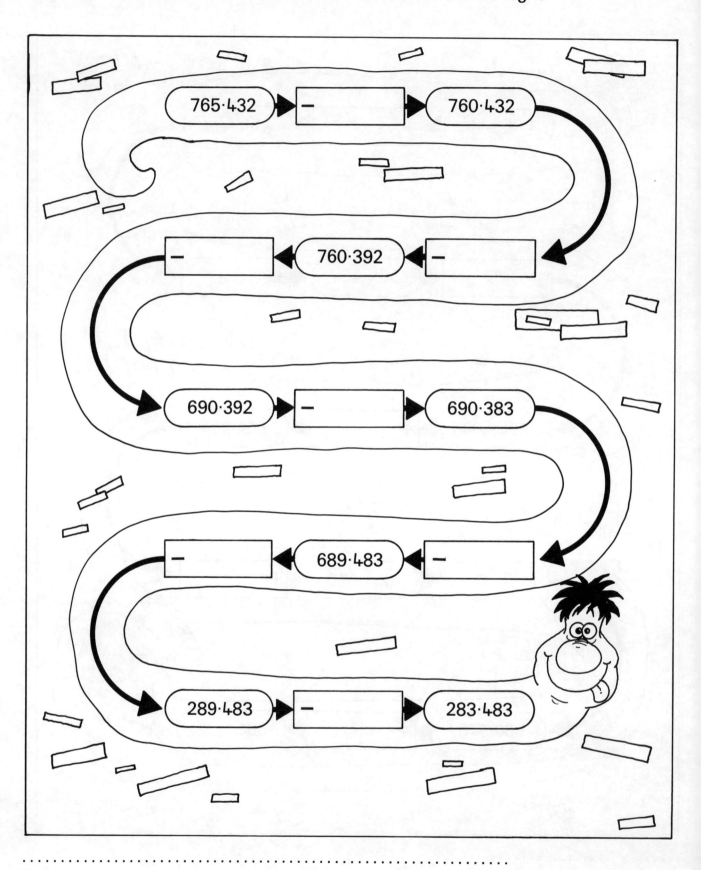

765·432 → − → 760·432

− ← 760·392 ← −

690·392 → − → 690·383

− ← 689·483 ← −

289·483 → − → 283·483

. . . .

Name _____ Class _____

DECIMAL PLACE VALUE: PRACTICE ACTIVITY (SUBTRACTION).

Twister (×)

Fill in the missing numbers in the boxes to make the twister right.

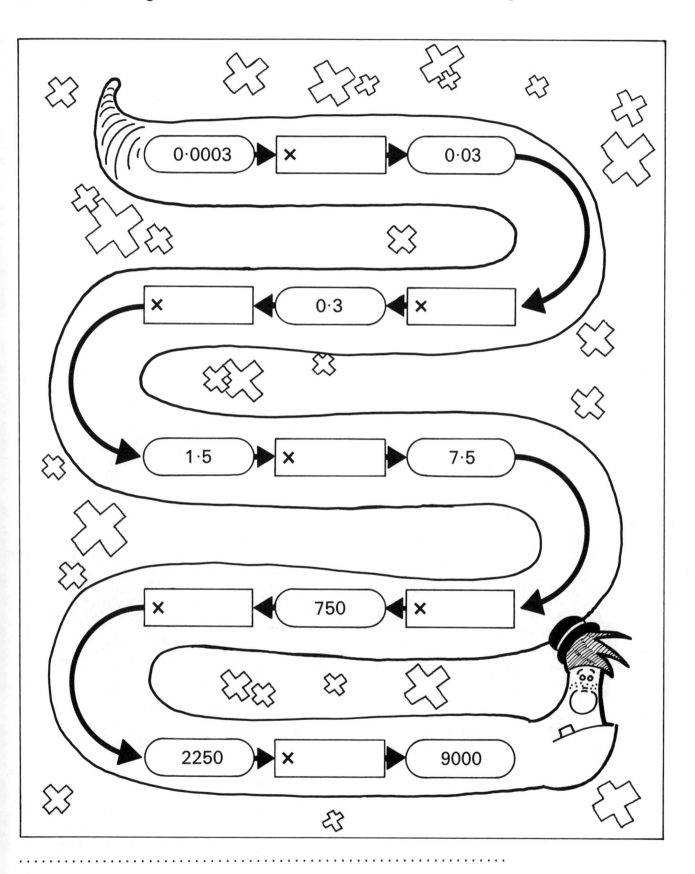

....

Name _____ **Class** _____

DECIMAL PLACE VALUE: PRACTICE ACTIVITY (MULTIPLICATION).

© Unwin Hyman
Calculated to Please 3

Twister (÷)

Fill in the missing numbers in the boxes to make the twister right.

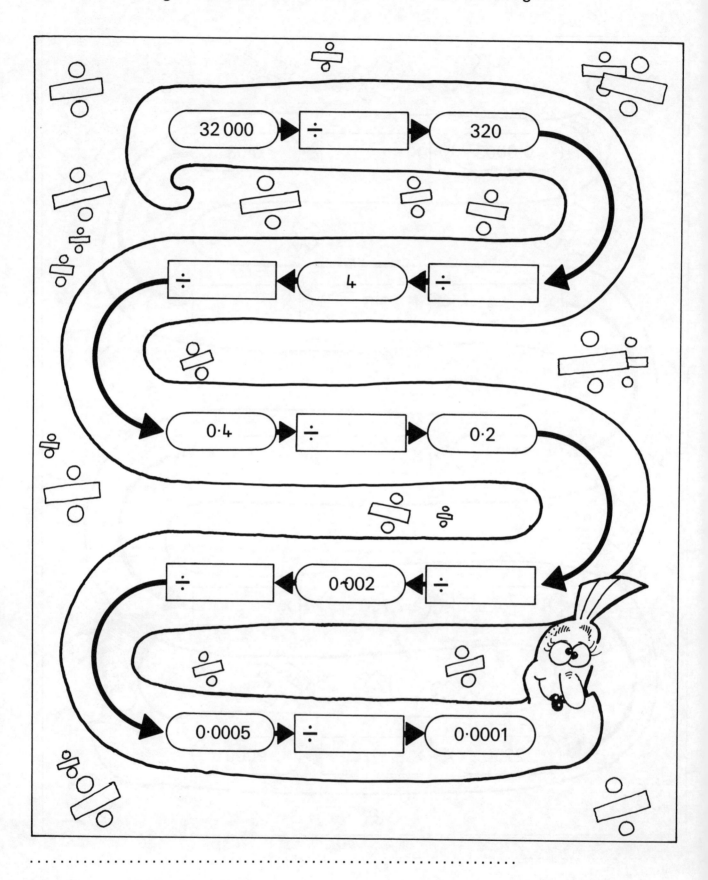

....

Name _____ **Class** _____

DECIMAL PLACE VALUE: PRACTICE ACTIVITY (DIVISION).

Twister

Fill in numbers to show a way to get from the **Start** number to the **End** number.

Be careful – the signs change!

Start: 2·7 + □

□ − □ ×

□ + □

□ ÷ □ −

□ + 0·12 End

....

Name _____   Class _____

DECIMAL PLACE VALUE ACTIVITY, USING THE FOUR RULES.

© Unwin Hyman
Calculated to Please 3

A bunch of three ㊽

Activity/Purpose

A game to develop skill in ordering fractions and decimals. Two
players compete to record three **consecutive** fractions/decimals
on the number line. A winning position would be, for example:

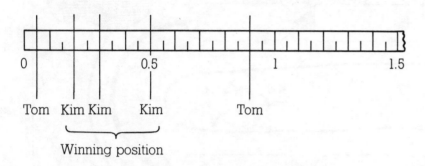

Winning position

Previous mathematical knowledge and skill required

Knowledge of simple fractions <2.
Ability to convert fractions to decimals by division.
Understanding of the structure of a number line.

Notes on using the page

Check understanding of the concept of a fraction as a ratio.
Ensure understanding of the rules, particularly that only a
sequence of **consecutive** marks wins the game.

EQUIPMENT

 1 calculator.

 Two different coloured
pencils or felt-tip pens.

Answers/Solutions

The sequence of given fractions is as follows, reading across:

$\frac{1}{20}=0\cdot05$	$\frac{1}{10}=0\cdot1$	$\frac{3}{20}=0\cdot15$	$\frac{1}{5}=0\cdot2$	$\frac{1}{4}=0\cdot25$
$\frac{3}{10}=0\cdot3$	$\frac{2}{5}=0\cdot4$	$\frac{9}{20}=0\cdot45$	$\frac{1}{2}=0\cdot5$	$\frac{3}{5}=0\cdot6$
$\frac{7}{10}=0\cdot7$	$\frac{3}{4}=0\cdot75$	$\frac{4}{5}=0\cdot8$	$\frac{9}{10}=0\cdot9$	$\frac{11}{10}=1\cdot1$
$\frac{6}{5}=1\cdot2$	$\frac{5}{4}=1\cdot25$	$\frac{13}{10}=1\cdot3$	$\frac{7}{5}=1\cdot4$	$\frac{15}{10}=1\cdot5$
$\frac{8}{5}=1\cdot6$	$\frac{17}{10}=1\cdot7$	$\frac{7}{4}=1\cdot75$	$\frac{18}{10}=1\cdot8$	$\frac{19}{10}=1\cdot9$

ADDITIONAL ACTIVITIES EXTENSIONS

1. Discuss any 'tricks' for a winning
   strategy.
2. Make an unnumbered 'blank' of
   the page and use it to:
   (a) extend the given fractions to
   thirds, sixths and ninths;
   (b) extend the given fractions to
   random selection.

Ⓝ Ⓞ Ⓣ Ⓔ Ⓢ

A bunch of three

(41)

A calculator game for 2 players.

Take turns to:

1. Choose and cross out a fraction on the grid.
2. Use a calculator to change it to a **decimal**.
3. Mark the decimal on the number line in your own colour.

The aim for each player is to get 3 marks next to each other.

The first to get **a bunch of three** is the winner!

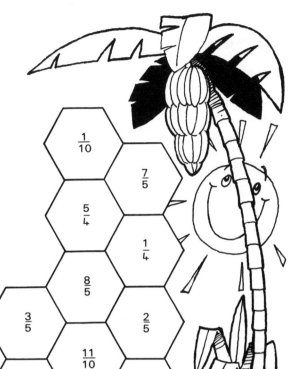

The fractions on the grid:

$\frac{1}{10}$ $\frac{7}{5}$ $\frac{5}{4}$ $\frac{1}{4}$ $\frac{8}{5}$ $\frac{3}{5}$ $\frac{2}{5}$ $\frac{7}{10}$ $\frac{11}{10}$ $\frac{1}{5}$ $\frac{3}{4}$ $\frac{1}{20}$ $\frac{9}{20}$ $\frac{3}{10}$ $\frac{1}{2}$ $\frac{17}{10}$ $\frac{19}{10}$ $\frac{6}{5}$ $\frac{18}{10}$ $\frac{9}{10}$ $\frac{3}{20}$ $\frac{7}{4}$ $\frac{15}{10}$ $\frac{4}{5}$ $\frac{13}{10}$

Number line marks: 0   0.5   1   1.5   2

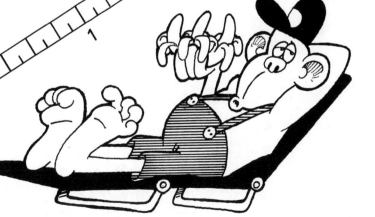

Name _____   Class _____

GAME: ORDERING FRACTIONS AND DECIMALS.

© Unwin Hyman
Calculated to Please 3

Divide and match ㊷

● ● ● ● ● ●

Activity/Purpose

The purpose of the activity is to generate related sets of decimals from given numerators and denominators. These are then used to find fraction families (i.e. equivalent fractions) and to observe and analyse other patterns according to the ability of the child.

Previous mathematical knowledge and skill required

Experience and understanding of a fraction as a ratio of two numbers.
Understanding of the terms **numerator** and **denominator.**
Ability to use the constant function for division.

Notes on using the page

Ensure that the child understands the terms numerator and denominator, and can 'read' on the grid the pairs of numbers to be divided.
Encourage the child to use the constant function for division in order to speed up the process of generating the decimals, e.g.:
$\boxed{8}\ \boxed{÷}\ \boxed{÷}\ \boxed{=}\ \boxed{0}$ followed by $\boxed{1}\ \boxed{=}$, then $\boxed{2}\ \boxed{=}$ ...
will produce the 'denominator of 8' row.

Families of equivalent fractions should be marked on the grid and could also be written elsewhere – perhaps on a wallchart.
Allow the pattern recognition to be conducted at the child's own level, with hints as necessary.

● ● ● ● ● ●

Answers/Solutions

See below.

ADDITIONAL ACTIVITIES EXTENSIONS

1. Encourage the child to find at least three more members of each 'fraction family' observed.

2. Use a decimal number line to 'place' sequences of decimals in their approximate position. This will show how each row is divided into spaces of equal size.

3. An able child may wish to extend the grid to the right and/or downwards, using squared paper.

	Numerator									
Denominator	**1**	**2**	**3**	**4**	**5**	**6**	**7**	**8**	**9**	**10**
1	1	2	3	4	5	6	7	8	9	10
2	0·5	1	1·5	2	2·5	3	3·5	4	4·5	5
3	0·3333333	0·6666666	1	1·3333333	1·6666666	2	2·3333333	2·6666666	3	3·3333333
4	0·25	0·5	0·75	1	1·25	1·5	1·75	2	2·25	2·5
5	0·2	0·4	0·6	0·8	1	1·2	1·4	1·6	1·8	2
6	0·1666666	0·3333333	0·5	0·6666666	0·8333333	1	1·1666666	1·3333333	1·5	1·6666666
7	0·1428571	0·2857142	0·4285714	0·5714285	0·7142857	0·8571428	1	1·1428571	1·2857142	1·4285714
8	0·125	0·25	0·375	0·5	0·625	0·75	0·875	1	1·125	1·25
9	0·1111111	0·2222222	0·3333333	0·4444444	0·5555555	0·6666666	0·7777777	0·8888888	1	1·1111111
10	0·1	0·2	0·3	0·4	0·5	· 0·6	0·7	0·8	0·9	1

42

Divide and match

To change a fraction to a decimal divide the numerator by the denominator.
Fill in the missing decimals in this grid.

Numerators

÷	1	2	3	4	5	6	7	8	9	10
1	1								9	
2	0·5		1·5		2·5			4		5
3	0·3333333		1						3	
4	0·25		0·75			1·5				
5	0·2				1		1·4		1·8	
6	0·1666666		0·5				1·1666666			
7	0·1428571			0·5714285					1·2857142	
8	0·125						0·875	1		1·25
9	0·1111111				0·5555555		0·7777777			
10	0·1				0·5					

Denominators

1. Find the fraction families which make the **same** decimal.
   Ring them in different colours.
2. Find other interesting number patterns.
   Write about them on the back of this page.

Name _____

Class _____

PATTERNS IN CALCULATOR-GENERATED FRACTION FAMILIES.

Repeaters 1 and 2

Activity/Purpose

The purpose of the activity is to use the rapid computational ability of the calculator to examine patterns of recurring decimals.

Previous mathematical knowledge and skill required

Experience of changing fractions (ratios) to decimals.
Ability to read several places of decimals.
Understanding of the terms numerator and denominator.

Notes on using the pages

The first page is a structured sequential investigation of patterns which emerge when numbers are divided by 9 and 99. The child is given a series of linked fractions and must record their decimal equivalents. Three statements are then completed, and these highlight the patterns which emerge.
It would be wise to check success on the first section before allowing the child to move on.
Encourage the child to make a good guess at the next 'answer' before using the calculator.

The second page investigates patterns of recurring decimals. It would be advisable to check the given examples and discuss the definition before proceeding. In particular the 'short' way of recording recurring decimals should be checked and emphasised to ensure understanding.

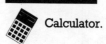

EQUIPMENT

Calculator.

ADDITIONAL ACTIVITIES EXTENSIONS

1. Encourage the child to find more examples of each type of 'repeater'. In particular, $\frac{1}{11}, \frac{2}{11}, \ldots$ and $\frac{1}{22}, \frac{2}{22}, \ldots$ are useful.

2. Extend the notion of recurring/ repeated decimals to other fractions. These are often beyond the scope of the calculator capacity (especially its display) but can be handled by 'normal' long division, (e.g. $\frac{1}{17}$ is a sixteen-digit repeat; $\frac{1}{13}$ is a six-digit repeat.

3. If available on the calculator, allow use of the reciprocal key $\boxed{^1/_x}$ for calculation of the unit fraction (numerator of 1).

Links with our own maths scheme

Other activities and extensions used

General evaluation of the children's work

Answers/Solutions

Repeaters 1

$\frac{1}{9} = 0.1111111$ $\frac{7}{9} = 0.7777777$

$\frac{2}{9} = 0.2222222$ $\frac{8}{9} = 0.8888888$

$\frac{3}{9} = 0.3333333$ $\frac{10}{9} = 1.1111111$

$\frac{4}{9} = 0.4444444$ $\frac{11}{9} = 1.2222222$

$\frac{5}{9} = 0.5555555$

$\frac{6}{9} = 0.6666666$

Number of digits in each denominator is **1**.

Number of digits repeated is **1**.

The repeated digit is the same as the **numerator** of the fraction.

$\frac{1}{99} = 0.010101$ $\frac{47}{99} = 0.474747$

$\frac{2}{99} = 0.020202$ $\frac{62}{99} = 0.626262$

$\frac{3}{99} = 0.030303$ $\frac{81}{99} = 0.818181$

$\frac{4}{99} = 0.040404$ $\frac{93}{99} = 0.939393$

Number of digits in each denominator is **2**.

Number of digits repeated is **2.**

The repeated digit is the same as the **numerator** of the fraction.

Repeaters 2

Single-digit repeat		Two-digit repeat		Three-digit repeat		Last-digit repeat	
Fraction	**Decimal**	**Fraction**	**Decimal**	**Fraction**	**Decimal**	**Fraction**	**Decimal**
$\frac{1}{3}$	$0.\dot{3}$	$\frac{1}{22}$	$0.04\dot{5}$	$\frac{1}{37}$	$0.\dot{0}2\dot{7}$	$\frac{1}{15}$	$0.0\dot{6}$
$\frac{1}{30}$	$0.0\dot{3}$	$\frac{1}{33}$	$0.\dot{0}\dot{3}$	$\frac{1}{111}$	$0.\dot{0}0\dot{9}$	$\frac{1}{18}$	$0.0\dot{5}$
		$\frac{3}{11}$	$0.\dot{2}\dot{7}$	$\frac{1}{54}$	$0.018\dot{5}$	$\frac{1}{24}$	$0.041\dot{6}$
				$\frac{132}{999}$	$0.\dot{1}3\dot{2}$	$\frac{1}{36}$	$0.02\dot{7}$
				$\frac{1}{222}$	$0.00\dot{4}\dot{5}$	$\frac{1}{12}$	$0.083\dot{3}$

No repeat	$\frac{1}{4}=0.25$	$\frac{1}{8}=0.125$	$\frac{1}{20}=0.05$	$\frac{1}{32}=0.03125$
	$\frac{1}{5}=0.2$	$\frac{1}{10}=0.1$	$\frac{1}{25}=0.04$	$\frac{1}{40}=0.025$

Repeaters 1

Change these fractions into decimals.

$\frac{1}{9}=$ ☐

$\frac{2}{9}=$ ☐

$\frac{3}{9}=$ ☐

$\frac{4}{9}=$ ☐

$\frac{5}{9}=$ ☐

$\frac{6}{9}=$ ☐

$\frac{7}{9}=$ ☐

$\frac{8}{9}=$ ☐

$\frac{10}{9}=$ ☐

$\frac{11}{9}=$ ☐

The number of **digits** in each denominator is ☐ .

The number of digits **repeated** in each decimal is ☐ .

The repeated digit is the same as the ☐
of the fraction.

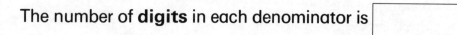

$\frac{1}{99}=$ ☐

$\frac{2}{99}=$ ☐

$\frac{3}{99}=$ ☐

$\frac{4}{99}=$ ☐

$\frac{47}{99}=$ ☐

$\frac{62}{99}=$ ☐

$\frac{81}{99}=$ ☐

$\frac{93}{99}=$ ☐

The number of **digits** in each denominator is ☐ .

The number of digits **repeated** in each decimal is ☐ .

The repeated digits are the same as the ☐
of the fraction.

Name _____   Class _____

CALCULATOR-GENERATED PATTERNS OF RECURRING DECIMALS.

© Unwin Hyman
Calculated to Please 3

Repeaters 2

When we change **some** fractions to decimals, some of the digits
after the decimal point are repeated again and again.
We say that they **recur**. They are **recurring decimals**.

Examples

Fraction	Display	Name	Short way to write
$\frac{1}{9}$	0 · 1 1 1 1 1 1 1	Single-digit repeat	0·1̇
$\frac{1}{11}$	0 · 0 9 0 9 0 9 0	Two-digit repeat	0·0̇9̇
$\frac{1}{6}$	0 · 1 6 6 6 6 6 6	Last-digit repeat	0·16̇
$\frac{1}{27}$	0 · 0 3 7 0 3 7 0	Three-digit repeat	0·0̇37̇

Change these fractions to decimals.
Record the fraction **and** the short way to write the decimal.

> Cross them out as you do each one!

$$\frac{1}{3} \quad \frac{1}{4} \quad \frac{1}{5} \quad \frac{1}{8} \quad \frac{1}{10} \quad \frac{1}{15} \quad \frac{1}{18} \quad \frac{1}{20} \quad \frac{1}{22} \quad \frac{1}{24}$$

$$\frac{1}{25} \quad \frac{1}{30} \quad \frac{1}{32} \quad \frac{1}{33} \quad \frac{1}{36} \quad \frac{1}{37} \quad \frac{3}{11} \quad \frac{1}{111} \quad \frac{1}{40} \quad \frac{1}{54} \quad \frac{132}{999} \quad \frac{1}{12} \quad \frac{1}{222}$$

Single-digit repeat		Two-digit repeat		Three-digit repeat		Last-digit repeat	
Fraction	Decimal	Fraction	Decimal	Fraction	Decimal	Fraction	Decimal

No repeat

....

Name _____ Class _____

CALCULATOR-GENERATED PATTERNS OF RECURRING DECIMALS.

© Unwin Hyman
Calculated to Please 3

Use your calculator

● ● ● ● ● ●

Activity/Purpose

The purpose of the activities is to encourage use of the calculator, in real measurement situations, as an aid to speed of computation. This allows concentration on the **process** of measurement.

Each page contains four measurement activities for two children to attempt together. They cover length, area, mass and weighing, and volume and capacity.

Previous mathematical knowledge and skill required

Experience of practical measurement activities.
An ability to estimate.
Familiarity with decimal notation and place value.

Notes on using the pages

The pages can be attempted in any order, and related to the current or recent work in your mainstream scheme. Each activity requires some personal measurement, or calculation based on personal measurement, or calculation based on personal data. Therefore children should be given the opportunity actually to measure the named items. Encourage the children to estimate first (*and* to make a note of the estimates!) before measuring. The amount of work produced will depend upon the ability of the children. Allow work at various levels to emerge.

● ● ● ● ● ●

Answers/Solutions

Because all the activities are based on measurement by the child, and in his or her own context, general answers are not possible. Assess the quality of the work produced by the child's ability to explain what has been done and to justify the answers achieved.

EQUIPMENT

 Calculator.

Metre sticks, 20-metre tape-measures, a trundle-wheel, rulers marked in mm, balance scales, bathroom scales, a measuring cylinder, a stop-watch. School atlas. Matchbox.

ADDITIONAL ACTIVITIES EXTENSIONS

1. Encourage discussion of the usefulness of calculators in practical measurement activities.
2. Encourage calculator use in general measurement activities.

Links with our own maths scheme

Other activities and extensions used

General evaluation of the children's work

Use your calculator – length

45

Work with a friend.

A double-decker bus is 4·27 metres high.

How many people of **your** height would need to stand on each other's **shoulders** to be able to see over the top?

Your fingernails grow at about 1 mm per week.

If you had never cut them, how long would your nails have been on your last birthday?

A penny has a diameter of 20·3 mm.

How much money would be raised if your school made a line of pennies from the door of the Head's room to your classroom door?

A mole can dig a tunnel 85 metres long in one day.

How many days would a mole need to dig a tunnel all around your school building?

Name _____

Class _____

USING A CALCULATOR IN MEASUREMENT ACTIVITIES: LENGTH.

© Unwin Hyman
Calculated to Please 3

Use your calculator - area

Work with a friend.

An unrolled roll of wallpaper has an area of 5·3265 m².

How many rolls would you need to wallpaper your classroom?

The world's largest book is the 'Super Book', published in Denver, U.S.A. When it is open, it measures 3·07 metres across and it is 2·74 metres high. What is its area?

How many open copies of your school atlas would cover the same amount of space?

The world's largest indoor stadium is in New Orleans, U.S.A. It has an area of 52 600 m².

How many classrooms the size of yours would fit into that stadium?

A postage stamp has an area of 5 cm².

How many would you need to cover the main door of your school?

Name _____   Class _____

USING A CALCULATOR IN MEASUREMENT ACTIVITIES: AREA.

© Unwin Hyman
Calculated to Please 3

Work with a friend.

A £1 coin has a mass of 9·5 grams.

How much money would you be worth if you were weighed in £1 coins?

Find the mass of your best friend in kilograms.

The world record for weight-lifting is about 480 kg.

How many people of the same mass as your friend could be lifted at the same time by the world champion?

The largest living land animal is the African elephant. Its mass is about 5600 kg.

Estimate whether this is more or less than the total mass of all the children in your school.

The largest apple grown in Britain had a mass of 1·357 kilograms.

How much heavier are you than that apple?

How many times heavier are you than that apple?

Name _____ Class _____

Work with
a friend.

Use a measuring
cylinder, a stop-watch
and a dripping tap!

How much water does
one dripping tap
waste in a day?

How many cups of
coffee would that
wasted water have
made?

A one litre can of
gloss paint will
cover 12 m² in
one coat.

How many millilitres
of paint would you
need to paint the **top**
of your desk or table?

What is the **volume**
of just one page of
your school atlas?

Calculate the **volume**
of a matchbox.

About how many
matchboxes would fit
into your desk or locker
or tray?

About how many
matchboxes would fit
into your classroom?

Name _____

Class _____

Teens

● ● ● ● ● ● ●

Set your calculator to [ ] like this: [ ][ ][ ][ ][=][0]

How many [ ]s must you [ ] to get from **Start** to **Finish**?

First make a **good guess** and ring the display where you **think** the **Finish** will be. Then fill in all the displays between the **Start** and **Finish** numbers, counting in [ ]s.

Good guess?

Finish at: | Start at:

1.

2.

3.

4.

5.

6.

7.

Name _____ Class _____

USING THE CALCULATOR CONSTANT FUNCTION TO DEVELOP ESTIMATION SKILL.

© Unwin Hyman
Calculated to Please 3

Talking calculators

●●●●●

Work with a friend.

Find as many upside-down 'words' as you can.

For each one, write a calculation that puts the word into the display.

Use this sheet to start you off with words starting with ☐ .

Word	Number	Calculation

You can write lists of words, numbers and calculations
for these starting letters.

B E G H I L O S Z

....

Name _____

Class _____

INVESTIGATING AND RECORDING UPSIDE-DOWN 'WORDS', NUMBERS AND
CALCULATIONS.

© Unwin Hyman
Calculated to Please 3